Praise for Plan B

"Lester Brown tells us how to build a more just world and save the planet...in a practical, straightforward way. We should all heed his advice."

—President Bill Clinton

"...a far-reaching thinker."

—*U.S. News & World Report*

"The best book on the environment I've ever read."

—Chris Swan, *Financial Times*

"It's exciting...a masterpiece!"

—Ted Turner

"[Brown's] ability to make a complicated subject accessible to the general reader is remarkable..."

—Katherine Salant, *Washington Post*

"In tackling a host of pressing issues in a single book, *Plan B 2.0* makes for an eye-opening read."

—*Times Higher Education Supplement*

"A great blueprint for combating climate change."

—Bryan Walsh, *Time*

"[Brown] lays out one of the most comprehensive set of solutions you can find in one place."

—Joseph Romm, *Climate Progress*

"...a highly readable and authoritative account of the problems we face from global warming to shrinking water resources, fisheries, forests, etc. The picture is very frightening. But the book also provides a way forward."

—Clare Short, British Member of Parliament

"Lester R. Brown gives concise, but very informative, summaries of what he regards as the key issues facing civilization as a consequence of the stress we put on our environment....a valuable contribution to the ongoing debate."

—*The Ecologist*

"Brown is impassioned and convincing when talking about the world's ills and what he considers the four great goals to restoring civilization's equilibrium..."

—April Streeter, *TreeHugger.com*

"In this impressively researched manifesto for change, Brown bluntly sets out the challenges and offers an achievable road map for solving the climate change crisis."

—*The Guardian*

"...the best summation of humanity's converging ecological problems and the best roadmap to solving them, all in one compact package."

—David Roberts, *Grist*

"Lester R. Brown... offers an attractive 21st-century alternative to the unacceptable business-as-usual path that we have been following with regard to the environment (Plan A), which is leading us to 'economic decline and collapse.'"

—Thomas F. Malone, *American Scientist*

"Brown's overall action plan is both comprehensive and compelling."

—Caroline Lucas, *Resurgence*

"Beautifully written and unimpeachably well-informed."

—Ross Gelbspan, author of *The Heat is On*

"The best single volume on saving the earth, period."

—Geoffrey Holland, author of *The Hydrogen Age*

The Great Transition

Earth Policy Institute® is a nonprofit environmental research organization providing a plan for building a sustainable future. The Institute issues regular updates that assess progress in implementing Plan B, available along with data and graphs on the EPI website.

Website: www.earth-policy.org

THE GREAT TRANSITION

Shifting from Fossil Fuels to Solar and Wind Energy

Lester R. Brown

with Janet Larsen, J. Matthew Roney,
and Emily E. Adams

EARTH POLICY INSTITUTE

W • W • NORTON & COMPANY

NEW YORK   LONDON

For information about permission to reproduce selections from this book, write to Permissions, W. W. Norton & Company, Inc., 500 Fifth Avenue, New York, NY 10110

For information about special discounts for bulk purchases, please contact W. W. Norton Special Sales at specialsales@wwnorton.com or 800-233-4830

Manufacturing by Courier Westford
Production manager: Louise Mattarelliano

ISBN: 978-0-393-35055-5

W. W. Norton & Company, Inc., 500 Fifth Avenue,
New York, N.Y. 10110
www.wwnorton.com

W. W. Norton & Company, Ltd., Castle House, 75/76 Wells Street,
London W1T 3QT

1 2 3 4 5 6 7 8 9 0

For Abby, Bittle, Bridget,
Cal, Cash, Lena, Mandolyn,
and young people the world over

Contents

Measurements in this book are typically U.S. Standard units, except for tons, which are metric. Expanded data sets and additional resources are available at www.earth-policy.org.

Preface

Energy transitions are not new. Beginning several centuries ago, the world shifted from wood to coal. The first oil well was drilled over 150 years ago. Today we are at the start of a new energy transition, one that takes us from an economy run largely on coal and oil to one powered by the sun and the wind. This monumental shift, which is just getting under way, will compress a half-century of change into the next decade.

The purpose of this book is to describe how this great transition is starting to unfold. While the book cuts a wide swath and takes a global view, it is not meant to be a comprehensive study of the world energy economy. Each technology discussed here easily deserves its own book, as do many topics important to the transition that are not discussed in depth here, such as energy efficiency, the "smartening" of electrical grids, energy savings opportunities in industry, and batteries and other energy storage.

One "hot" technology, hydraulic fracturing—or fracking, as it is commonly known—has turned around declining production curves for oil and gas in the United States. Hailed for creating an energy revolution, fracking is also assailed for its disruption of human lives and the environment around each of the thousands of new wells being drilled each year. In this book we aim to give a sense of some of the trends that are creating a real energy revolution, not a short-term fix.

The sun is the primary source of energy. The world has long been dependent on fossilized sunlight in the form of coal, oil, and natural gas—the result of millions of years of heat and pressure on ancient organic material. On the one hand, these are exceptional fuels, extraordinarily dense with energy. Yet they are incredibly dirty, climate-disruptive, and ultimately exhaustible. Our descendants will one day shake their heads in wonder at how we could so quickly extract and burn up this inheritance—marring landscapes, clouding the skies, and destabilizing the earth's climate in the process.

The great energy transition is a move away from fossil resources in favor of cleaner, non-depletable sources of energy. We focus primarily on solar and wind because of their low cost, rapid growth, and enormous potential. Every country can get energy from the sun or the wind, and each passing year it is getting cheaper to do so. Regardless of how much solar and wind energy we use today, it does not reduce the amount available tomorrow. Once the investment in solar installations or wind turbines is made, the fuel is free. Increasingly, Wall Street investors and savvy governments are recognizing this basic reality.

Fossil fuels have been heavily subsidized through government spending and tax policy, as well as more indirectly through their effects on our health and the environment—costs that society bears. The good news is that coal consumption may have peaked in China as public discontent over air pollution there has grown to the point where the social cost of coal can no longer be ignored. If coal consumption continues to fall in China, which today uses more coal than all other countries combined, this fuel source may fade at the global level far faster than anyone imagined.

Nuclear power, whose cost is also distorted by enormous subsidies, can be ruled out by economics alone. Indeed, nuclear's flawed economics are largely responsible for the decline in global nuclear electricity generation that began nearly a decade ago. Meanwhile, solar and wind power installations are multiplying at a blistering pace. Solar and wind electricity generation records at both the state and the national level are regularly surpassed. Although the playing field remains unbalanced, wind and solar costs are falling so rapidly that they are starting to squeeze out coal.

While the cost of electricity from geothermal power plants has not fallen as fast, geothermal energy is an important source of baseload power generation in areas with an abundance of underground heat. It also can ramp up quickly when the sun sets or the wind slows. Hydropower—currently the largest source of renewable energy by far—plays the same role. But for most of the world, the era of large dam building is over. The 1.3 billion people still without electricity can get power from solar panels faster and at a far lower cost than from large hydropower projects, and with much less social disruption.

One source of renewable energy that we do not cover is plants—namely biomass along with ethanol, biodiesel, and other plant-based transportation fuels. Biomass burned in power plants currently generates three times more electricity than solar, but it is growing far more slowly: 7 percent annually over the last three years versus 60 percent for solar.

The potential for biomass is limited. Plant material is far less energy-dense than fossil fuels. Given the great amount of energy that goes into producing plant-based fuels, the energy profits are narrow. And cars are ravenous consumers: filling the tank of a large SUV one time with ethanol takes as much grain as could feed a person for a whole year. Even if the vast U.S. corn crop were turned into ethanol, it would meet only 18 percent of American gasoline demand. Thus this book proposes shifting the transportation system from liquid fuels to electricity. Given the global food situation, with close to a billion people undernourished and with farmers struggling to expand output fast enough to keep up with demand, the world will not be able to divert major land and water resources to energy production. Wind and solar projects win out here because, unlike fossil fuel or nuclear power plants, they do not require massive amounts of water for cooling, and their footprints on the land can be small.

As we were wrapping up this book at the close of 2014, a year that was shaping up to be the hottest on record—a record the world keeps breaking anew with alarming frequency—we realized that we are in a race. It is a race between tipping points. Can the world's economies move to wind and solar fast enough to avoid crossing key thresholds that could cause climate change to spiral out of control? Or will we continue down a dead-end street, trying to eke every last hydrocarbon out of the ground until we are all cooked?

The old energy economy was tightly controlled by those who held fossil fuel deposits. The new energy economy is much more democratic. The wind and the sun can be tapped wherever people live. *The Great Transition* provides glimpses of this new energy economy that is just starting to emerge.

Earth Policy Institute
January 2015
1350 Connecticut Ave. NW, Suite 403
Washington DC 20036
Phone: (202) 496-9290
epi@earth-policy.org
www.earth-policy.org

The Great Transition

1

Changing Direction

The worldwide transition from fossil fuels to renewable sources of energy is under way. As fossil fuel resources shrink, as air pollution worsens, and as concerns about climate instability cast a shadow over the future of coal, oil, and natural gas, a new world energy economy is emerging. The old economy, fueled largely by coal and oil, is being replaced with one powered by solar and wind energy.

We can now see this new economy starting to take shape. We saw it in 2013, when Denmark generated 34 percent of its electricity from the wind. In January 2014, wind supplied a whopping 62 percent of that country's electricity. Portugal and Spain each got over 20 percent from wind in 2013, and Ireland, 17 percent. Indeed, on some days wind power supplies half of Ireland's electricity. In Spain, wind is challenging nuclear power to become the country's leading source of electricity. And for several days in August 2014, electricity generated from wind in the United Kingdom eclipsed that from coal.

We also see the new economy surfacing in the state of South Australia, where wind farms now supply more electricity than coal plants do. On September 30, 2014,

[handwritten margin notes: Wind energy very successful in many European countries]

[handwritten bottom note: Wind overtaking older energy solutions in many countries]

power generation from the wind and the sun exceeded the state's electricity demand. In China, electricity from wind farms has surpassed that from nuclear power plants. And water for 170 million Chinese households is heated by rooftop solar water heaters.

In the United States, the start of the energy transition is on display in the hundreds of utility-scale solar power plants under development or construction in the Southwest. And Iowa and South Dakota are each generating at least 26 percent of their electricity from wind farms. The wind share in Iowa could reach half by 2018. Texas, which now gets nearly 10 percent of its electricity from wind power, is building huge wind farms and the long-distance transmission lines that will facilitate the sale of low-cost wind-generated power in Louisiana and Mississippi.

Solar and wind costs are falling fast, undercutting fossil fuels in a growing number of electricity markets. A July 2014 study by the Danish government projects that new wind farms coming online there in 2016 will supply electricity at half the cost of that from new coal and natural gas plants. In parts of Australia, which is experiencing a solar boom, the cost of producing electricity from the sun has fallen well below that from coal. In fact, a 2014 analysis citing government data reported that high electricity delivery costs mean that coal-fired power still could not compete with solar, even if the coal itself were free.

The energy transition is advancing rapidly in some unexpected places. Falling costs for solar and wind energy are opening the door for massive investments in Africa. Bloomberg New Energy Finance reported in August 2014 that there would be more renewable energy installations in Africa in 2014 than during the preceding 14 years. Wind and solar projects in Latin America are advancing even faster.

[margin handwritten notes] Very cost effective

Cheap enough for developing nations

Several concerns are driving the great transition from fossil fuels to renewables. One of these is climate change and its effect on our future. Another is the health impact of breathing air polluted by burning fossil fuels, as seen in the 3 million people who die each year because of outdoor air pollution. A third is the desire for local control over energy production and overall energy security.

In response to these broad-based public concerns, government policies—including emissions controls, renewable energy targets, and financial incentives—are encouraging the shift to renewables, principally solar and wind. And as the need for clean alternatives to coal and oil is becoming apparent, there is growing interest in solar and wind energy within the investment community. This includes not only investment banks but also several billionaires who are plowing vast sums of money into renewable energy. The influx of "smart money" into this relatively new segment of the energy economy suggests that much more investment will likely follow.

As scientists have been pointing out for decades, carbon dioxide (CO_2) emissions from burning coal, oil, and natural gas are altering the climate. Increasing levels of CO_2 and other greenhouse gases in the atmosphere are raising the earth's temperature. The consequences include melting ice sheets and glaciers, rising sea level, worsened drought in some areas, more intense rainfall in others, and more-destructive storms. If the world continues to rely heavily on fossil fuels, the global average temperature could rise by nearly 11 degrees Fahrenheit (up to 6 degrees Celsius) by the year 2100. Melting ice and the thermal expansion of the oceans could raise sea level by some 6 feet during this century.

The stakes are high, and there is no need to look beyond food security to see why. A Stanford University study analyzed the historical relationship between temperature and corn yields from some 600 U.S. counties. It concluded that each 1 degree Celsius rise in temperature above the growing-season norm dropped yields 17 percent. Wheat and rice, the world's food staples, are similarly vulnerable to higher temperatures. Viewed against the projected 6 degree rise in temperature during this century, which would bring more crop-withering heat waves, shrinking harvests could drive food prices up to unprecedented levels, resulting in chaos in the world food economy.

The rise in sea level threatens to inundate Asia's highly productive rice-growing river deltas, including the vast Ganges Delta in India and Bangladesh and the Mekong Delta in Viet Nam. Because so much rice is grown in low-lying river deltas, this world food staple is uniquely vulnerable to the rising global temperature.

Beyond the rice fields of Asia, rising sea level also poses a serious threat to some of the world's most populous cities, including New York, Tokyo, London, Shanghai, and Mumbai. Residents in these cities will have to decide whether to "stay and fight"—by building dams, levees, and other protective structures—or move to higher ground. The costs to society of the combined effect of rising food prices and urban inundation could bring the world economy to its knees.

Time is everything. We cannot turn back the clock and prevent the earth's temperature from rising. That is already happening. But if we move to dramatically cut carbon emissions with a wartime sense of urgency, we may be able to slow the rise and prevent climate change from spiraling out of control. This means restructuring the world energy economy: saying farewell to fossil fuels, embracing efficiency, and quickly expanding the use of renewable forms of energy.

Encouragingly, the energy transition is progressing much faster than most people realize. And it will accelerate. We are looking at the prospect of a half-century's worth of change within the next decade. Whereas the cost of energy from fossil fuels is largely commodity-dependent and will increase over time as the fuels become more scarce, producing power from the wind and the sun is largely technology-dependent, with costs falling as the science improves. Every country has its own supply of renewable energy. Both solar and wind energy are widely distributed and also inexhaustible. In contrast to coal and oil, the amount of solar and wind energy consumed today does not reduce the amount available tomorrow.

The worldwide use of solar cells to convert sunlight into electricity is expanding by over 50 percent a year. Early photovoltaic (PV) installations were typically small-scale—mostly on residential rooftops. Now, in addition to millions of rooftop installations, thousands of utility-scale solar projects are under development or construction.

At peak power, the solar systems installed worldwide by the start of 2014 could match the output of at least 100 nuclear reactors. As technology progresses and as PV system costs fall, the accelerating spread of rooftop installations—both residential and commercial—is reducing the market for utility-generated electricity in many communities. With their market shrinking, utilities are forced to adapt or raise prices. Yet higher prices encourage the installation of even more solar panels. Once under way, this cycle can reinforce itself, leading to what is commonly described as a "death spiral" for electric utilities.

more PV
↗
higher utility costs

This scenario has recently played out in Germany, where leading utilities including the giants RWE and E.ON found themselves at risk of bankruptcy, in part because rooftop solar installations were satisfying a growing share of residential needs and driving down wholesale power prices. Now these utilities are retooling their business models to better accommodate renewables in order to survive in the new energy landscape. A similar situation could unfold in the sun-rich U.S. Southwest, where the number of rooftop installations is growing exponentially.

With solar panel costs continuing to fall and with the number of installations multiplying, installing solar panels on residential rooftops in villages in developing countries is now often cheaper than building a central power plant and the grid to supply electricity. Just as cell phones took off in the developing world and bypassed reliance on the traditional network of landline telephones, rooftop solar generators are bypassing the electric grid.

Numerous other trends are signaling the fast-moving shift from fossil fuels to renewable sources of energy. The burning of coal, for example, is declining in many European countries. In the United States, the number two coal consumer after China, coal use dropped 18 percent from 2007 to 2013 as scores of coal-fired power plants closed.

Of the 500-plus U.S. coal plants that were generating electricity at the beginning of 2010, fully 180 have closed or are scheduled to do so, leaving 343 plants in operation. Among the reasons for this drop are local opposition to coal (often for health and environmental reasons), the adoption of stricter air quality regulations that raise the price of coal-fired power, the growing use of solar and wind energy, and the rapidly expanding availability of low-cost natural gas. A strong force in the U.S. anti-coal movement is the Sierra Club's Beyond Coal campaign. Its goal is to close all the coal plants in the country by 2030, replacing them with a combination of efficiency gains and clean energy.

Thus far, an increased reliance on natural gas has helped the United States begin to wean itself from coal. The burgeoning use of horizontal drilling and hydraulic fracturing or "fracking" techniques to coax trapped oil and natural gas out of shale rock formations reversed a decline in U.S. natural gas production, boosting it 32 percent between 2006 and 2014. Yet while it has been touted as a "bridge fuel" to a clean energy economy, natural gas is losing its luster. In producing energy, burning natural gas emits only half as much CO_2 as coal. However, recent studies have found that in many cases natural gas can actually be worse for the climate because of the extensive leakage of methane—a much more potent greenhouse gas—from wells, pipelines, and tanks.

Ultimately, since gas reserves are limited and new wells are depleted so rapidly, it makes little sense for society to invest in expanding the gas infrastructure and then have to abandon it. This would simply become another dead-end street, a diversion from building a lasting energy economy. While natural gas and oil prices are volatile, dependent on an unpredictable supply from exhaustible reserves, there is no fuel cost for wind and solar installations. Zero.

When looking at the decline in coal burning in the United States and many other industrial countries, the question that inevitably arises is, But what about China, which uses more coal than all other countries combined? The good news is that coal use in China started to fall in 2014. "Peak coal" is nigh. Two deeply held concerns in Beijing will bolster China's nascent energy transition. One is the effect of coal burning on the health of the Chinese people and the resulting political unrest that it brings. The other is the scarcity of water, which is needed in large quantities to mine coal, to wash it, and to cool coal-fired power plants.

As for oil, the other major source of global CO_2 emissions, its use is fading in many industrial countries—including in the leading consumer, the United States. American oil consumption dropped 9 percent from 2005 to 2013. Part of this is due to people driving less and part is due to the development of ever more fuel-efficient cars. Oil use can be reduced even further by increasing mass transit options and by electrifying the transport system and then powering it with solar- and wind-generated electricity. Plug-in hybrid and all-electric cars can run largely on carbon-free electricity. And since powering cars with wind-generated electricity costs roughly the equivalent of $1-per-gallon gasoline, the market will help drive the transition to electric cars.

Oil companies are facing growth constraints on both the supply and the demand sides of the energy equation. Demand is weakening as vehicles become more efficient and as motorists look to alternatives to driving. Meanwhile, on the supply side, remaining oil reserves are less accessible than the large gushers found in decades past, making it more costly to bring new oil to market.

Among those losing out in the energy transition are the big independent oil and gas companies, including Chevron, ExxonMobil, and Shell—three of the giants in the field. These three firms combined spent a half-trillion dollars between 2009 and 2013 to expand oil and gas production, but even with this hefty investment, their production declined in 2013. Each company suffered a drop in profits that year.

The stock market has not been kind to Big Oil. While the Standard & Poor's (S&P) 500 Index rose 54 percent from the beginning of 2012 through the third quarter of 2014, shares of Chevron and ExxonMobil rose only 12 and 11 percent, respectively, and those of Shell rose just 4 percent.

The financial and logistical risks of expanding oil production are substantial. As conventional fields are depleted and the new finds are smaller or more dispersed, such as oil trapped deep beneath the ocean floor or in tar sands or shale, extracting and processing oil uses

the oil business is struggling

more energy than ever before. Tapping it requires costly equipment and experienced engineers, who are becoming harder to find. In late 2013 and early 2014, Chevron, Shell, and ExxonMobil each announced cuts in capital spending. These firms may soon have to do something that large corporations are not accustomed to doing—namely, start shrinking their operations.

Oil companies are faced with soaring production costs in many situations. After spending more than $6 billion trying to develop oil resources off of Alaska without a drop of oil to show for its efforts, Shell announced in January 2014 that it was suspending efforts to drill there. Accompanying the announcement was the release of data showing that the company's profits for the fourth quarter of 2013 had fallen by 71 percent. Its new chief executive officer, Ben van Beurden, also announced that Shell was cutting its capital expenditures from $46 billion in 2013 to $37 billion for 2014, a reduction of 20 percent. Then in August 2014, Shell—seemingly determined to throw good money after bad—again submitted plans to the U.S. government to drill off the coast of Alaska.

Another prime example of escalating costs is the Kashagan field below the Caspian Sea, where a consortium that includes ExxonMobil, Shell, Total, and Eni is drilling for oil. Kashagan was found in 2000—the world's largest oil discovery in 30 years, though still a far cry from the giant deposits in the Middle East. It also has become the costliest. As difficult conditions have forced a series of delays, the cost of bringing oil to market has soared from the early estimate of $10 billion to $50 billion spent as of late 2014. The cost is likely to climb further, illustrating yet again that the low-hanging fruit in the oil sector has already been picked.

The oil industry is much more dependent on government handouts than is generally realized. In 2013, governments worldwide subsidized the fossil fuel industry with over $600 billion, giving this aging industry over five times the $120 billion that went to renewables. About half of the fossil fuel subsidies went to boost oil consumption. In effect, taxpayers' money is being used to subsidize climate change.

For the first time in their careers, oil company CEOs are being forced to lower their production goals and expectations simply because the earth has been carefully picked over during a century of intense international oil exploration and production. New oil finds are now barely sufficient to offset depletion. Failing to see the transition coming, CEOs are now behind the curve and without a game plan. They could have decided to broaden their portfolios and become energy companies, becoming part of the transition instead of being overrun by it.

Why did they adopt an ostrich-like head-in-the-sand approach by denying that an energy transition was under way? Indeed, companies like ExxonMobil and Shell have recently argued that the world will continue to remain heavily dependent on oil and that anyone who thinks otherwise is dreaming. Their solution to whatever problems that a restructuring of the energy economy poses for them has been to vociferously deny its existence while simultaneously using their financial and political muscle to fight it and maintain their relevance.

It now seems apparent that if the world takes climate change seriously, much of the oil still underground will never be used. As journalist Kieran Cooke wrote for the Climate News Network, "if any meaningful action is to be taken on climate change in the years ahead, the activities of the fossil fuel industry will have to be severely curtailed and the bulk of assets frozen, inevitably leading to a sharp decrease in corporate valuations—what some analysts refer to as a bursting of the 'carbon bubble.'"

Much of the remaining coal, oil, and natural gas will become what are called "stranded assets." Public attention was drawn to the concept of stranded assets in the context of climate change by Carbon Tracker, a U.K.-based nonprofit, in a 2011 report entitled *Unburnable Carbon*. Drawing on research by the Potsdam Institute, the group observed that for the world to have a chance of constraining the global average rise in temperature to 2 degrees Celsius, as the international community has agreed to do, it will need to dramatically reduce fossil fuel use. According to the latest scientific estimates, to have decent odds of staying within that 2 degree Celsius limit, the world will need to limit the CO_2 emitted from the remaining underground fossil fuels in the first half of this century to 1,400 gigatons (1 gigaton equals 1 billion tons). And since we had already released 400 gigatons of CO_2 by 2013, only 1,000 gigatons can be released between 2013 and 2050.

The CO_2 embodied in the world's remaining proven fossil fuel reserves total 2,860 gigatons in the form of coal (roughly 65 percent), oil (22 percent), and natural gas (13 percent). If only 1,000 gigatons can be burned under the 2 degree warming scenario, that means 1,860 gigatons worth of carbon reserves, mostly in coal and oil, must be left in the ground. In this case, the reserves lose value and become stranded assets. This requires recalculation of the worth of energy companies that have included these assets in their valuations. Stockholders want to know what their energy stocks are worth.

Throughout history, economic transitions have left stranded assets in their wake. Think of the shift from whale oil to kerosene. Or from the horse and buggy to the automobile. This energy transition is no exception. It will leave behind a wealth of stranded assets. Coal companies are among the most obvious losers. As U.S. coal consumption dropped from 1,023 million tons in 2007 to 839 million tons in 2013, scores of coal mines were idled and coal power plants were closed. In addition to unusable coal reserves, power plants, and mines, stranded assets related to the coal industry will include special railroads that once linked mines to the market as well as coal handling and storage facilities at rail depots and ports.

Coal is not alone. The giant French energy firm Total announced in May 2014 that it and its partners were putting on hold a tar sands mining operation in Alberta, Canada, one in which they had already invested $11 billion. The cost of producing the oil was too high to warrant additional investment. This huge project could very well become a stranded asset.

Fossil fuels are not the only bastions of the old energy economy that are losing in the competition with low-cost renewables. World nuclear electricity generation, which was seen as the power source of the future a half-century ago, is declining as costs climb. Electricity from new nuclear power plants can cost twice as much as solar- and wind-generated electricity. Nuclear power will continue to fade into the past as aging plants, many too costly to maintain and operate, are closed.

The worldwide decline of nuclear electricity generation that began in 2006, then driven primarily by economics, is now also driven by fear of accidents. The 2011 Fukushima nuclear meltdown in Japan is helping to lower the curtain on the nuclear era. Immediately after Fukushima, German Chancellor Angela Merkel ordered seven of the country's oldest nuclear power plants to shut down. Two months later the government announced a complete nuclear phaseout by 2022. Germany plans to replace nuclear plants largely with wind- and solar-generated electricity. Other countries in Europe and elsewhere also reassessed their nuclear plans.

[handwritten margin note: solve countries are ending nuclear power production completely]

The two countries most often cited as nuclear power successes are France, which gets 75 percent of its electricity from nuclear plants, and China, the leader in building new plants. But that story is about to change. While France is completing construction of its last nuclear plant, it is in the process of developing 25,000 megawatts of wind generating capacity, of which 8,300 megawatts were already online in 2013. It is aiming to drop its nuclear share of power to 50 percent by 2025. China, which has 16,000 megawatts of nuclear generating capacity, has developed a world-leading 91,000 megawatts of wind generating capacity. Wind is leaving nuclear power in the dust.

One reason for wind's explosive growth in China is that wind farms scale up to a size not seen with coal-fired units or nuclear reactors. China is building several wind mega-complexes as part of its Wind Base program, each of which will have up to 6,800 megawatts of generating capacity. These projects are part of an effort to develop a path-breaking 200,000 megawatts of wind capacity by 2020.

While nuclear plants can take a decade to get up and running, wind farms typically go up within a year. (And a simple rooftop solar array can go up in one day.) In some parts of the world, wind is emerging as a leading component of the new energy economy. At the start of 2014, wind farms—now producing electricity in some 90 countries—had a generating capacity of 318,000 megawatts. China and the United States are currently the world leaders, with Germany, Spain, and India rounding out the top five.

These are some of the countries where the transition is under way, countries where stranded assets will become highly visible. They include coal mines, uranium mines, oil fields, oil refineries, deep water drilling rigs, oil pipelines, and gasoline service stations. In 1994, there were nearly 203,000 gas stations in the

United States, either free-standing or associated with convenience stores. As of 2013, fewer than 153,000 of these outlets remained, marking a decline of one fourth over the 19-year span. With electric or plug-in hybrid electric cars now starting to replace gasoline-powered cars, this shrinkage in the number of gas stations seems certain to continue.

One of the key questions is how fast plug-in hybrids and all-electric cars will take over the market. Chairman of the advisory board for Bloomberg New Energy Finance Michael Liebreich projected worldwide electric car sales would hit 300,000 in 2014. While this is less than 1 percent of total auto sales, he believes they are "in the process of passing through the credibility barrier." If so, the low fuel and overall operating costs of electric cars could drive their future sales steadily upward at the expense of gasoline-powered cars, further weakening the demand for oil.

Today the United States has more than 3,000 electric utilities, but a decade from now the electricity landscape will likely look very different. Some utilities will be forced to merge; others will be dismantled as rooftop panels take over more and more of the electricity market. Coal companies in the United States will become few and far between. Eventually, deep-water drilling firms will disappear simply because oil from beneath the ocean floor will be too costly to compete.

A combination of geological, economic, and social trends is speeding up the energy transition. One social movement aiming to accelerate it further is the fossil fuel divestment campaign. Student and community groups are pressuring university endowments and pension funds to restructure their investment portfolios to eliminate fossil fuel holdings. The idea is to publicly disavow support for climate-disrupting sources of energy. Stanford University was among the first schools with a large endowment to announce that it would get rid of all its coal industry stocks. The Rockefeller Brothers Fund, whose original resources ironically came from John D. Rockefeller, an early oil tycoon, announced in September 2014 that it was ditching all the fossil fuel stocks in its portfolio.

As more and more investors realize that investing in coal, oil, and natural gas companies is neither consistent with their philosophy nor economically promising, the current wave of divestment is likely to continue. The Smith School of Enterprise and the Environment at Oxford University looked at the potential "stigmatization" effect the divestment campaign could have on the images and reputations of corporations. At some point, the public resistance to coal and other fossil fuels could reach a point where anyone owning, managing, or lending to a coal company would risk damage to their public image and reputation.

The divestment movement is responding to the stark reality that climate change has begun. As each new extreme weather event reminds us, avoiding a major disruption to life as we know it depends on dramatically reducing carbon emissions to keep global warming in check. This requires a total restructuring of the global energy economy. It must be done quickly. Previous energy transitions—like that from wood to coal—took decades, but the bulk of this new energy transition must be condensed into the next 10 years. The shift from coal, oil, and natural gas to solar and wind energy will be the defining event of our era.

The bottom line is that solar and wind, which are abundant and increasingly cheap, will be the foundation of the new energy economy. During the fossil fuel era, investments were short term, yielding energy only until the oil wells went dry or the coal deposits were depleted.

The discovery-development-depletion cycle was repeated over and over again. Now, for the first time since the Industrial Revolution began, we are investing in sources of energy that can last as long as the earth itself.

Data, endnotes, and additional resources can be found at Earth Policy Institute, www.earth-policy.org.

2

The Rise and Fall of Oil

It was like a scene out of a science-fiction movie: a raging fire surrounded by water. But this was not on some imagined planet. It was in the Gulf of Mexico on April 20, 2010, when the Deepwater Horizon oil rig caught fire and 11 crew members lost their lives. Over the next three months, the world watched as try after try failed to staunch the flow from the blown-out well. Finally, on July 15th BP and the U.S. Coast Guard managed to cap the well sitting about one mile below the sea surface, but not before more than 4 million barrels of oil had spilled into the Gulf ecosystem, contaminating it for years to come.

The Deepwater Horizon disaster illustrates the great risks the industry is taking to feed the world's oil addiction. Tapping early oil finds was practically as easy as sticking a straw in the ground and watching black gold flow out. Now the era of easy oil is over.

Oil production is constrained by geology. Each of the major fields discovered between 1940 and 1980 held more than 10 billion barrels of oil. Saudi Arabia's mighty Ghawar contained 75 billion barrels. Those days are gone. New finds today are few and far between. Now a discovery is considered large if it contains more than 3 billion barrels of oil. Production is also constrained politically. About 80 percent of the remaining oil reserves are held by national oil companies, those that are partially or completely owned by state governments, such as Saudi Aramco and Russia's Rosneft. Most of those reserves are conventional oil sitting in large underground fields. That leaves 20 percent of the remaining bounty for the private companies, including the majors like BP, ExxonMobil, and Total, along with smaller independent companies.

Exploration and development costs are climbing as oil companies are forced to turn to ever less accessible locations. Future prospects for conventional oil development include oil fields beneath the ocean floor and others scattered about the Arctic Ocean, where drillers must contend with floating icebergs and some of the harshest weather on earth. Turning to unconventional resources, such as oil locked in shale rock formations or mixed with sand and clay in tar sands, is another option. But bringing hard-to-get oil to market is not cheap.

Ed Crooks of the *Financial Times* writes that "as companies pursue the ever more challenging oil reserves that they need to increase or merely sustain their production, their costs have risen to the point that the most expensive projects, such as deep water development... need an oil price of at least $100 a barrel to be commercially viable." As John Watson, Chief Executive Officer of Chevron, puts it, "One hundred dollars per barrel is becoming the new $20, in our business."

One of the richest finds in decades, the Kashagan oil field in Kazakhstan under the northern Caspian Sea, was discovered amid a lot of excitement in 2000. It is estimated to contain 35 billion barrels of oil, of which about 13 billion may be recoverable. But conditions are difficult. Sea ice forms in the winter, when temperatures can drop to 22 degrees below zero Fahrenheit. To make matters worse, the oil is mixed with deadly and corrosive hydrogen sulfide gas.

The oil companies in the consortium developing Kashagan—including ExxonMobil, Shell, Total, and Eni— have thus far spent $50 billion attempting to bring the oil field online. In 2013 the consortium finally started pumping, but this only lasted for a couple of weeks until a gas leak was discovered. After restarting briefly, it was closed down again, this time for much more extensive repairs. Pumping is set to resume in 2016, although some analysts are skeptical that it will happen even then. The Kashagan find is now known flippantly as "Cash-all-gone."

One area where unconventional oil is now being pursued is in Canada's oil sands, mostly located in Alberta Province. Also known as tar sands because of their semi-solid state, this viscous mixture of bitumen (a thick oil-based hydrocarbon), sand, clay, and water cannot be simply drilled and pumped. The easiest way to get it is to dig pit or strip mines, destroying the landscape. But many of the remaining deposits are now too far below the surface to use this method. Oil companies are using a technique to heat the bitumen underground to make it fluid enough to be pumped to the surface. Then more processing is required to make the tar sands oil ready to flow through a pipeline. The intensive production process requires a lot of energy. In fact, each unit of energy that goes into extracting and refining the tar sands yields just 5 units of energy. This poor energy return on investment is a far cry from the 16 or more units of energy yielded from pumping oil in conventional fields. Tar sands accounted for more than half of Canada's oil production in 2013.

In the United States, horizontal drilling and hydraulic fracturing ("fracking") in shale rock to get to previously inaccessible oil and gas have created an energy boom. Talk of "peak oil" has been replaced with talk of a shale revolution. Led mainly by smaller independent oil companies instead of the big majors, fracking has increased U.S. oil production to over 10 million barrels per day in 2013, up from less than 7 million in 2008. The deposits are so diffuse that many wells have to be drilled, yet they dry up quickly—far faster than conventional wells. Like any boom, this will one day go bust.

Because of the rising costs of access to resources, oil companies are pulling back on several fronts. Shell has cut back on shale drilling in the United States. After suffering several setbacks, Shell also temporarily suspended its Arctic drilling endeavors off the coast of Alaska, though it could resume attempts in 2015. Shell, France's Total, and Norway's Statoil have all stopped certain tar sands projects in Canada. Chevron has postponed an offshore drilling project in Indonesia. It has also lowered its overall oil production projections.

JBC Energy Markets in Vienna reports that while investment in pursuing oil and gas resources by the six largest oil companies rose 80 percent from 2007 to 2013, their oil and gas output fell 6 percent. This reversal in fortune is occurring against a backdrop of the growing use of oil. World oil consumption in 1983 totaled 58 million barrels per day. By 2013, it had climbed to 91 million barrels a day, an increase of 58 percent over 30 years. The United States, the world's leading oil consumer, uses nearly 19 million barrels of oil a day. Next come China, Japan, and India, which together consume another 19 million barrels daily. Following those countries are Russia, Saudi Arabia, Brazil, South Korea, Canada, and Germany.

In many emerging economies, including Brazil, China, India, and Indonesia, which have a combined population of 3.1 billion people, oil use is climbing steadily. In fact,

Indonesia was a member of OPEC, the Organization of Petroleum Exporting Countries, until its domestic oil use outpaced its production. Many other areas in Asia have seen tremendous growth in oil use. Hong Kong, Malaysia, Singapore, and Thailand have each almost tripled their oil use since 1990. China's oil use grew more than fourfold. Viet Nam increased its oil use more than fivefold. But although global oil use is still climbing, in a growing number of industrial countries oil use has peaked and begun to decline. For example, Germany's oil consumption peaked in 1979 at 3.3 million barrels per day, then dropped to 2.4 million in 2013, a decline of 29 percent. In Japan, daily oil use peaked in 1996 at 5.8 million barrels. Since then, it has declined to 4.6 million barrels a day in 2013, a drop of 22 percent. And even in the United States, following decades of growth, oil use is now falling.

From 1950 to 2005, U.S. oil use rose more or less continuously, with only occasional interruptions, such as the 1970s oil price shocks. Between 1950 and 2005, daily U.S. oil consumption climbed from 6 million barrels to 21 million barrels, more than tripling. It then peaked, with consumption falling to 19 million barrels per day in 2013—a drop of 9 percent in eight years.

Several trends help explain how oil use by the world's largest consumer started to fall. With most oil used for transportation, two thirds of which goes to move passenger cars and trucks, changes in vehicle use and the way vehicles are powered translate into large changes in oil consumption.

During the twentieth century, the car played a central role in defining the American lifestyle. It became an integral part of U.S. culture. Cars not only provided unprecedented mobility, they helped define the people who owned them. Automotive historian John Wolkonowicz summed up the situation: "For people who grew up and lived in the twentieth century, the car was freedom, it was status, it was an extension of you, a visible expression of you and your personality."

By the year 2000, the United States found itself with over 190 million licensed drivers and an even larger car fleet. It was consuming some 20 million barrels of oil per day—at that time, more than the next five countries combined. But now the United States, the country that led the world into the automobile age, is showing signs of leading it out.

The most basic ways to reduce gasoline use are by driving less and by driving more efficiently. Driving less means more people commuting by bike, on foot, or by public transportation or sometimes just working from home. That leads to people owning fewer cars. Driving more efficiently results from vehicle technology improvements, often prompted by government-mandated standards. The big efficiency jump comes from switching from the internal combustion engine to electric motors.

These shifts are starting to happen in the United States. Michael Sivak, who tracks automotive trends at the University of Michigan, points out that the annual distance traveled by solo drivers in the United States dropped 9 percent between 2004 and 2011. Some of the reasons for this were uncovered in an analysis for the U.S. PIRG Education Fund based on Census Bureau data. In 61 percent of the urban districts surveyed, the use of public transit has increased. The survey also found that a growing share of the workforce is working from home. Strikingly, in 99 percent of districts surveyed, the share of workers commuting by private vehicle declined. Indeed, the Federal Transit Administration measured a 20 percent increase in the number of people using public transportation in the United States between 2000 and 2011.

For American teenagers in rural communities a half-century ago, getting a driver's license and something to drive—a car, a pickup, even a farm truck—was a rite of passage. That's what everyone did. Today's teenagers socialize much more through smartphones and the Internet. For many of them a car is of little interest. Twenty years ago, 68 percent of American teenagers had a driver's license at the age of 18. Today 59 percent do.

Michael Sivak writes that "it is possible that the availability of virtual contact through electronic means reduces the need for actual contact among young people." Ashley Halsey III, a reporter for the *Washington Post*, makes a similar point: "American teenagers seem to get no thrill from driving in an electronic age when their friends are a finger tap away 24-hours a day, an era when Twitter, Instagram and texting have displaced the mall and the malt shop as hangouts."

It is not just teens abandoning car culture. Data from the National Household Travel Survey indicate that the entire under-35 demographic is driving less. The number of miles driven by those younger than 35 fell by an impressive 23 percent between 2001 and 2009.

Phineas Baxandall, a senior analyst at the U.S. PIRG Education Fund, notes: "Government should support transportation initiatives that support these travel trends. Instead of wasting taxpayer dollars continuing to enlarge our grandfather's Interstate Highway System, we should invest in the kinds of transportation options that the public increasingly favors." This would result, for example, in a greater focus on such things as expanding public transit and creating more bike lanes.

Some cities around the world, recognizing the extra pollution, noise, and congestion an expanding car fleet brings, have begun to restrict the use of automobiles. In certain places this is done with an entry fee charged when cars enter the city center. Cities like Singapore, London, and Stockholm have implemented such a "congestion charge." Chinese cities feeling the pressure from the fast-growing car fleet are also trying to limit the rise of the auto. Shanghai began auctioning license plates in 1994. There, a license plate can easily cost more than the car. Beijing, Tianjin, Guangzhou, Guiyang, and Hangzhou have also imposed limits on the number of cars sold. Other Chinese cities are likely to follow.

After a certain point, more cars in a city mean less mobility and a diminished quality of life. In earlier times, urban transport was designed around cars. Now this is changing. The last few decades have seen hopeful new signs in the design and management of cities. Forward-thinking communities are beginning to plan their transport systems so that more residents have ready access to public transport and it is easier to walk and bike.

Cities around the world are also developing more parks and trails where people can walk and enjoy the outdoor environment. The ratio of parks to parking lots in a community is one of the best indicators of its livability. Cities that have many parks are pleasant places not only to walk, jog, and bike, but also to live. Those that have mostly parking lots designed to facilitate the use of cars are not nearly as attractive.

Recent years have also witnessed a surge of interest in bicycles and in their place in the transport system. Bicycles are competing with cars for short-distance travel. In the United States, bike commuting expanded 38 percent nationwide over the last decade. Cycling is growing fast in large cities like Baltimore, Chicago, Minneapolis, Philadelphia, and Portland, Oregon—all places where it has at least doubled since 2000. These cities have worked to encourage bicycling.

Portland, one of the most bike-friendly cities in the United States, has installed over 400 miles of bikeways and now has racks for more than 5,500 bikes. Cycling rates have grown threefold since 2000. But even here, only 6 percent of the workforce commutes to work by bike. Compare this with Copenhagen, Denmark's capital, where 36 percent of the workforce commutes by bike—a share that is still growing.

U.S. sales of bikes and cars are nip and tuck. Over the last decade, the sale of new bikes, excluding those for children, has been remarkably stable, hovering around 13 million a year. In 2012, this put them close on the heels of new-car sales of 15 million. Whenever a bike trip replaces one by car, it reduces air pollution, carbon emissions, and traffic congestion.

In Europe, where annual bicycle sales have hovered around 20–21 million, bike sales exceed car sales in virtually every country. Italy sold more bikes than cars in 2011, marking the first year this had happened since World War II. Climbing bicycle sales in Spain reached 780,000 in 2012—eclipsing car sales of 700,000.

Owning a bike is no longer a requirement for riding in many cities thanks to bike-share programs. In the United States, by the end of 2012 some 21 cities had 8,500 bikes in bike-share racks. By the end of 2015, this is expected to climb to over 70 cities with close to 40,000 bikes. The Washington, D.C., metro area, an early American leader, has more than 300 bike-share stations with close to 3,000 bicycles at the disposal of 18 million annual visitors and the residents of the District of Columbia and its neighboring suburbs.

Bike-sharing programs have sprung up worldwide in recent years. More than 700 cities in 57 countries now have fully operational bike-share programs. Europe has the most programs, but Asia has more bikes to share.

Perhaps not surprisingly, the leader in fleet size is China, which now has over half a million shared bikes. The reasons for adopting bike-sharing programs vary from city to city. Consider New York's Citi Bike program that launched with 6,000 bikes in May 2013. It greatly increases mobility but costs very little. Janette Sadik-Khan, New York's Commissioner of Transportation, said, "Citi Bike isn't just a bike network; it's New York City's first new public transit system in more than 75 years." Bike-sharing programs are often designed to complement bus and rail systems, dealing with what planning officials call the "first mile/last mile" problem. In Hangzhou, China, where bicycles are highly popular, the city launched the bike-sharing program to facilitate connections by public transit riders on both ends of their trips.

Bike-sharing is even being put to use by General Motors (GM), one of the world's leading automobile manufacturers. GM has an agreement with a bike-share start-up company called Zagster to provide bikes to GM's 19,000 employees on its 300-acre GM Tech Center in Warren, Michigan. What's more, Bill Ford, the head of Ford Motor Company, is investing in Zagster through a venture capital firm. Tim Ericson, the 28-year-old CEO of Zagster says, "We're creating what is almost becoming a citywide bike sharing program, with no public funds and no use of public space."

Corporations, universities, and local governments are all participating in the bicycle renaissance. The World Bank, at its headquarters in Washington, D.C., fosters biking by providing changing rooms, showers, hair dryers, and a secure bike parking area.

The economic attractions of cycling are compelling. Bicycles not only save fuel, they also save land because 20 bikes can fit in the parking spot for one car. The 250 million cars in the United States require some 800 million parking spaces. Adding parking together with road infrastructure, Americans' auto addiction has led to the paving of at least 61,000 square miles, an area larger than the state of Illinois.

Substituting a bike for a car reduces materials use—steel, aluminum, plastic, and rubber—from 4,000 pounds to 30 pounds. And of course there is the accompanying reduction in energy use in the manufacturing of these materials. It also benefits taxpayers simply because the road maintenance required for a bicycle is minuscule compared with that for a car.

The combination of biking, walking, and public transit options found in well-designed cities can give urban residents a great advantage: car-free living. The share of carless households increased in 84 out of 100 U.S. urban areas surveyed between 2006 and 2011. And as urbanization increases, this share will only rise.

After growing rapidly throughout the twentieth century and into the early years of this century, car numbers in some countries have plateaued over the last several years. For example, between 2001 and 2007 the number of licensed vehicles in the United States climbed from 217 million to close to 250 million. During the next seven years, this number has fluctuated narrowly around the 250 million mark. It is only a matter of time until the fleet slowly begins to shrink as the younger, less car-oriented generation gets older.

Europe's automobile fleet is not growing either. Indeed, new-car registrations are near a 20-year low. Several reasons for this include high fuel prices, longer-lived vehicles, slippage in the car as a status symbol, and the fact that fewer young people are getting a driver's license.

In Japan, car sales have shrunk in recent years. This is partly because of the high cost of operating and parking vehicles and partly because the population is aging. These factors make it likely that the automobile fleet will begin to decline there.

With their high car ownership rates, industrial countries have a large potential for shrinking their car fleets. In the United States, there are 786 cars for every 1,000 people, including children too young to drive and adults who no longer do so. Italy, with 682 cars per 1,000 people, is not far behind. For both Germany and Japan, the number is 588. France follows closely with 582. Other countries with at least one car for every two people include Poland, Spain, and the United Kingdom.

Far on the other end of the car ownership scale are places where fleets are expanding. Ethiopia has just 3 cars for every 1,000 people. In Brazil, with 210 cars per 1,000 people, the car fleet doubled since 2003 to reach over 80 million cars as the middle class expanded and the government supported car buying. India had car sales of 2.5 million in 2013. It is projected to become the third largest car market in the coming years, dramatically boosting its car ownership rate of 18 per 1,000 people.

China, with 69 cars per 1,000 people, overtook the United States as the world's largest market for new cars in 2009. New-car sales in China reached 18 million in 2013, slightly higher than America's top sales year of 17.8 million in 2000. It is clear that if China were to have three cars for every four people, as the United States does, they would have roughly a billion cars—as many as there are in the whole world today. Long before this level of automobile ownership is reached in China, rising pollution and congestion will make it obvious that having a "car in every garage" is not a dream but a nightmare.

Worldwide, in 1980 there were 320 million licensed cars on the road. By 2012, this number had more than doubled to 770 million. But even with car sales climbing in emerging markets, growth at the global level is slowing. Some analysts expect the world fleet to peak within the next few years.

Helping to hasten that peak is the rise of car-sharing. Car-sharing programs are expanding rapidly in many parts of the world. They reduce the need for automobile ownership by allowing members short-term use of a car, sometimes for trips measured in minutes. Many of today's drivers simply want access to a car when they need it. Unwilling to be burdened with the responsibilities of vehicle registration, insurance, fueling, parking, and maintenance, not to mention the cost of buying a car, they are turning to car-sharing operations such as Zipcar, Car2Go, Enterprise CarShare, and others. Zipcar, in addition to being found in large U.S. cities, is available on over 250 college and university campuses.

The Frost and Sullivan research group projects that the 3.5 million drivers enrolled in car-share programs worldwide in 2013 will soar to 26 million by 2020. As of 2013, some 39 percent of car sharers were in Europe and 10 percent were scattered across Asia. An analysis in North America, home to just over half of the world's car-share members, concluded that each car-sharing vehicle removed at least nine privately owned vehicles from the street. Other estimates go as high as each shared car replacing 32 private vehicles. In the United States, 1.2 million car-share members participated in 24 programs in 2013, with a total of 17,000 vehicles. One bonus of car sharing is that as people get used to doing without their own car, they tend to drive less overall.

Another development that will reduce oil use is that new cars hitting the road have the potential to be far more efficient than the ones headed for the scrapyard. In the United States, for instance, this will be accelerated because the federal government set ambitious fuel efficiency standards for new cars. In 2013, the average new car sold was getting roughly 24 miles per gallon (mpg). By 2025, this will rise by mandate to 54 mpg. During a 12-year span, the distance a new car can travel on a gallon of gasoline will more than double.

The big jump in efficiency will come from the growing prevalence of electric cars. It is beginning with plug-in hybrids that can run on both gasoline and electricity, such as the Toyota Prius Plug-in Hybrid now on the market. Still in the early stages, hybrid-electric and fully electric cars now cost more than those burning gasoline, but over time their cost will decline. Analysts at the global financial services firm UBS expect battery costs, a major portion of an electric vehicle's price tag, to be cut in half by 2020. This will make it feasible to substitute the highly efficient electric motor for the wasteful internal combustion engine, which produces more heat than traction. The rule of thumb is that an electric motor is three times more efficient than an internal combustion engine.

Norway is the unquestioned national leader in the transition to an electrically powered vehicle fleet, with a goal of 50,000 zero emissions vehicles on its roads in a matter of years. At the start of 2014, the best-selling vehicle in Norway was the Tesla Model S, an all-electric car. The government is providing strong incentives for electric car owners, including free road tolls, free parking, and free charging stations. Electric vehicles are also exempt from the high tax levied on conventional vehicle purchases. This strong, broad-based package that is simultaneously encouraging the use of electric cars while discouraging the use of gasoline or diesel is making for a fast transition.

Some automotive market analysts are beginning to think that the transition to an electrically powered transport system will come much faster than widely expected. As this shift proceeds, the source of the electricity to power the cars becomes increasingly important. If the vehicle gets its electricity from a rooftop solar installation or a wind farm, this would make it carbon-free. Running a car on electricity costs roughly the equivalent of $1 per gallon. For most Americans, plugging their car into the existing grid will already produce fewer greenhouse gas emissions than filling it up with gasoline would. A transportation sector powered largely with solar- and wind-generated electricity is not yet in full view, but it is taking shape. We can see it coming.

For developing countries still in the early stages of building their transport systems, the smart path—for public health, for urban livability, and for the climate— is not to maximize the number of cars on the road but rather to maximize mobility. At some point the current oil-based transport system will prove untenable, either because of increasing traffic congestion and urban air pollution or because the geological and political constraints surrounding oil production will come to a head. The new goal is to jump quickly to a diversified and electrified transport system that is powered by locally available solar and wind energy.

Data, endnotes, and additional resources can be found at Earth Policy Institute, www.earth-policy.org.

3

Closing Coal Plants

We may wake up one morning in the not-too-distant future and realize that the world has reached a tipping point on coal. Use of this fuel will be declining worldwide, as it already is in many countries. Coal accounts for some 40 percent of global electricity generation. Natural gas accounts for 22 percent, hydroelectric power provides 16 percent, nuclear power some 11 percent, and oil just 5 percent. Wind, biomass, and solar make up the remainder. No one knows exactly when coal will lose its top ranking as a source of electricity, but with world solar generating capacity growing in recent years at a phenomenal 60 percent annually and wind by more than 20 percent, use of the black rock that led the world into the industrial age may decline even faster than many in the energy field expect.

Coal takes a heavy toll in each phase of its journey from the ground to the smokestacks of power plants and beyond. For coal miners themselves, the price is all too often black lung disease. Official data show that 76,000 coal miners have died in the United States since 1968 from black lung disease, a preventable affliction caused by breathing coal dust—a disease for which there is no cure. In China, with many more mines and less safety oversight, 10 times as many people are thought to be living with black lung disease today, though because of underreporting, the number could be far greater. More directly, accidents in Chinese mines have claimed over a thousand lives in each of the past several years.

Miners' deaths are only the beginning of coal's health burden. Coal burning is a major source of mercury—a potent neurotoxin—in the environment. In the world's water bodies, mercury travels up the aquatic food chain and endangers human health via fish consumption. Coal also contains lead, cadmium, arsenic, and other carcinogens that can enter the environment where coal is mined, washed, or burned. Breathing the sulfur dioxide, nitrogen dioxide, and particulate matter released to the air from burning coal increases a person's risk of cardiovascular and respiratory diseases, including heart attacks and lung cancer.

In the United States, air pollution from coal-fired power plants is estimated to cause more than 13,000 premature deaths each year, mostly in the coal-dependent eastern swath of the country. Coal pollution is implicated in triggering over 20,000 heart attacks and 217,000 asthma attacks annually. These figures are actually improvements over years ago, before regulations like the federal Clean Air Act and state laws reduced air pollution from coal plants, mostly by requiring scrubbers on smokestacks. The Clean Air Task Force estimates that such rules saved some 11,000 lives each year between 2004 and 2010. But there is still work to be done.

The death toll from bad air is famously high in China, where rates of cancer and cardiovascular diseases in severely polluted areas are soaring. *New York Times* Beijing correspondent Edward Wong writes: "Residents of its boom cities and a growing number of rural regions question the safety of the air they breathe, the water they drink and the food they eat. It is as if they were living in the Chinese equivalent of the Chernobyl or Fukushima nuclear disaster areas." A recent study by Teng Fei at Tsinghua University estimated that coal burning led to 670,000 early deaths in China in 2012 from strokes, coronary heart disease, lung cancer, and chronic obstructive pulmonary disease.

A Chinese government policy that gave communities north of the Huai River free coal to burn in boilers for heating created an unintentional experiment, allowing researchers to compare the longevity of people in areas with and without heavy coal use. Controlling for other factors, they found that the 500 million people living north of the river were paying a disturbingly high price for the free coal: their life spans were cut by an average of five years.

Until recently, conventional wisdom held that coal burning was at least an economic source of electricity. But a 2011 study led by Harvard Medical School professor Paul Epstein concluded that from the ground to the power plant, coal indirectly costs the U.S. economy an astounding $345 billion per year, largely because of the associated health care burden from air pollution and because of the climate change impacts. This massive figure exceeds the market value of the coal itself. In other words, the indirect costs to society of coal use are greater than the direct costs. Incorporating these indirect costs would easily double or triple the price of coal-generated electricity, making lower-cost wind and solar electricity clear winners.

In late 2013, U.N. Secretary-General Ban Ki-moon urged the world to take much stronger measures to stabilize climate, describing it as "the greatest single threat to peace, prosperity, and sustainable development." Hardly a week goes by without another dramatic example some-where in the world of how the changing climate is altering lives. Instead of discussing climate change in the future tense, now the discussion is all too often in the present tense. Any effort to stabilize the earth's climate starts with closing coal plants simply because they are the leading source of carbon emissions worldwide.

Countries are taking different approaches to wean themselves from coal. Europe has been on a downward trend for coal use since the mid-1980s. Since 1965, Ger-many—Europe's heaviest coal user—has cut its coal con-sumption in half. Meanwhile, in the United Kingdom and France coal use fell by 70 percent. France plans to close 15 coal plants with a collective generating capacity of 3,900 megawatts between 2012 and 2016 while at the same time expanding wind farms to 25,000 megawatts.

Denmark banned new coal-fired power plants in 1997 and is looking to phase out coal power entirely by 2025. In late 2010, Hungary announced it would close its one remaining coal plant. Some coal facility shut-downs have come about in creative ways. In March 2014 police closed a coal plant in the Savona district in northern Italy. A judge had ruled in favor of Savona's chief prosecutor, who cited a study that found emissions from the plant between 2000 and 2007 led to 400 premature deaths and 2,000 cases of heart and lung disease. The 660-megawatt coal facility will not be polluting the area any longer.

Outside of Europe, South Africa—the world's sixth largest coal user—has reduced coal use 9 percent since its peak in 2008. A carbon tax set to begin in 2016 will likely bring coal use down even further. In New Zea-land, releasing carbon into the atmosphere became more expensive following the introduction of an emissions trading scheme in 2008. Since then, coal use there has dropped by 30 percent.

Canada's Ontario Province, home to 39 percent of the country's population, had closed 16 of its 19 coal-fired plants by the end of 2012. Already the benefits are visible. In 2005, the province had 53 smog days. In 2013, there were only 2. Closing the province's huge Nanticoke Generating Station brought a reduction in carbon dioxide emissions that was equal to taking 3.7 million cars off the road. By April 2014, the three remaining coal plants were closed, making Ontario coal-free. At the same time, more than 25,000 homes, farms, schools, churches, and businesses either installed or started making plans to install small-scale, grid-connected photovoltaic arrays. The development of locally abundant wind resources is also playing a key role in Ontario's transition to renewable energy. For Canada as a whole, coal use has dropped more than a third since 2007.

In the United States, the number two coal user after China, coal use dropped 18 percent from 2007 to 2013. Of the 523 coal-fired power plants in the country, 180 either have recently closed or are scheduled to do so. One collateral benefit of this—in effect, a carbon reduction bonus—is the decline in the diesel fuel used by trains that carry the coal from mines to power plants across the country. The American Association of Railroads reports that the amount of coal moving by rail has been declining since 2008.

News headlines tell the story of coal's worsening prospects. In November 2013, the *Washington Post* ran an article entitled "Tennessee Valley Authority to Close 8 Coal Fired Power Units." When one of the leading institutions in developing coal-fired power in the United States turns its back on this energy source so dramatically, coal plant investors and owners throughout the country pay close attention.

An April 2013 *Washington Post* on-line headline read "Study: The Coal Industry Is in Far More Trouble Than

Anyone Realizes." The story covered a peer-reviewed study by three researchers at the Nicholas School of the Environment at Duke University. Among other things, the Duke team noted that if the U.S. coal industry were forced to comply with stricter regulations on controlling pollutants, costs would be prohibitive. Considering prevailing low natural gas prices, many operating plants would be forced to close.

This is starting to happen. For example, dozens of aging U.S. coal plants are likely to be retired in the near future due to a 2015 deadline requiring compliance with mercury and toxic air emissions standards set by the U.S. Environmental Protection Agency (EPA). The EPA has also started a process leading to regulations on carbon dioxide emissions, signaling to power producers that they should consider carbon in their long-term plans.

In many cases, closing the coal plants and replacing them with low-cost solar or wind energy or energy efficiency improvements is cheaper than retrofitting the plants.

In the northeastern United States, support for closing coal plants is mounting, and it cuts across many segments of society. In New Hampshire, for example, some 90 businesses are urging Public Service of New Hampshire, the local utility, to close both of its remaining coal power plants. Vermont and Rhode Island are both coal-free already.

At the start of 2013, seven utility-scale coal plants were still operating in New England. To feed these facilities, located in Connecticut, Massachusetts, Maine, and New Hampshire, the region spent $95 million in 2012 on coal imports, some from other states and some from other countries. Beyond this, the cost to operate and upgrade the aging fleet of coal plants to meet regulations is soaring. This is not just a matter of environmental acceptability but also of financial viability. Shifting from coal to solar and wind would benefit the local economies not only because of lower-cost electricity but also because the dollars spent would remain within the area.

Massachusetts, the most populous New England state, is planning the end of its coal era. Of the state's three remaining utility-scale coal plants that were operational in early 2014, one—Salem Harbor Power Station—closed on June 1, 2014. A second, Mt. Tom, ceased operation on the following day. The third, Brayton Point, is scheduled to close in 2017. At that point, Massachusetts will be coal-free. Closing coal plants has helped Massachusetts cut its carbon emissions by 21 percent since 2005, making it an example for the world to follow.

Further south, the large 480-megawatt GenOn coal plant in Alexandria, Virginia, across the Potomac River from Washington, D.C., closed in late September 2012. U.S. Representative Jim Moran called the plant "one of 200 dinosaurs built before 1960 and exempt from the Clean Air Act." The facility emitted copious amounts of nitrogen and sulfur dioxide and 72 pounds of mercury each year. Moran noted that "one seventh of a teaspoon of mercury dropped in a lake can poison that lake."

Across the country, California—which burns little coal within its borders—reduced the amount of coal-fired electricity that it imports from other states by 18 percent from 2007 to 2012. The state utility of Nevada plans to be coal-free by 2025. It has announced that it will shutter its coal-fired power plants, replacing them with wind farms, solar installations, and natural gas power plants.

Indeed, natural gas is the energy source that some utilities have been choosing to cut their power plant pollution. With the growing use of horizontal drilling and hydraulic fracturing ("fracking"), U.S. natural gas production has boomed in recent years. The increase in production has led to a drop in prices for the fuel, which in turn lures utilities away from coal. But natural gas is only a short-term stopgap. Like coal, gas is a depletable resource, one whose full environmental damage is slowly being uncovered. In areas with heavy natural gas development, air quality has deteriorated from the drilling and the concomitant boost in heavy machinery and trucking. The fracking process requires large quantities of water. Injecting fracking fluids that contain chemicals into the ground to create fissures in shale rock formations to free up natural gas puts valuable groundwater at risk of contamination. Complaints of health problems associated with the bad air and water have increased. Fracking and injection of wastewater, which sometimes contains radioactive elements, back into the ground have caused earthquakes in unlikely places, like Ohio and Oklahoma. On top of these problems, recent research suggests that methane leaks all along the supply chain can make natural gas even more climate-disrupting than coal. Over 400 U.S. municipalities have passed anti-fracking measures because of environmental, health, and seismic concerns. Yet the boom continues.

In February 2009, in her State of the State address, Governor Jennifer Granholm of Michigan drove home the benefits of moving away from both coal and natural gas: "Instead of spending nearly $2 billion a year importing coal or natural gas from other states we'll be spending our energy dollars on Michigan wind turbines, Michigan solar panels, Michigan energy-efficiency devices, all designed, manufactured and installed by... Michigan workers." In a state where half of the electricity comes from coal plants, this would be a big transition.

In some areas, the high water demands of coal-fired power plants may lead to their demise. This is a particularly lively issue in Texas, a water-stressed state that has nearly 30 coal plants either operating or in the permitting stage. Key water users in Texas have banded together to oppose coal plant construction. The unusual coalition includes farmers, thirsty cities, and environmentalists. As Ryan Rittenhouse, who works with Public Citizen's anti-coal campaign in Texas, points out: "Water is where [coal plants] are most vulnerable."

Matthew Tresaugue, writing in the *Houston Chronicle*, noted that "the clash is the result of rising demand for both water and energy in Texas. With the state's population expected to double by 2060, there will be more neighborhoods, more businesses, more lights, and more air conditioners. Meanwhile, the water supply is projected to decrease by 18 percent because of aquifer depletion and sediment accumulation in reservoirs, according to state forecasts."

Even with the tight water situation in Texas, planning for a new coal plant in Matagorda County, wittily called the White Stallion Energy Center, was moving ahead until growing opposition from a variety of local constituencies led the developer to abandon its proposal in February 2013. Rice farmers, who depend heavily on water, had worried that the power plant would squeeze them out of business. Environmentalists and fishers were concerned because of the additional mercury burden. Local people also feared the loss of water sustaining the estuaries that support nurseries for fish and shrimp and that provide a vital habitat for wintering birds. On its cancellation, the Sierra Club noted that "since the plant was proposed in 2008, the Texas electricity market has shifted substantially, with wind power and natural gas driving electricity prices so low that huge, capital-intensive new coal plants could not compete."

The Sierra Club—with its 2.4 million members and supporters—has become a leader in the effort to eradicate coal use in the United States. Spurred to action by the call for a coal rush in the Bush Administration's 2001 energy plan, the Sierra Club has coordinated a fight to prevent construction of new plants through its Beyond Coal campaign. As of late 2014, the organization, working with more than 100 other groups, had defeated proposals for 183 new coal plants and helped drive the announced retirement of 180 coal-powered plants.

With each extreme weather event—mega-storm, flood, or heat wave—that is associated in the public mind with climate change, the pressure to close coal plants intensifies. In response to a lawsuit brought by the Sierra Club and other organizations, Portland General Electric agreed to close Oregon's only remaining coal plant by the end of 2020. When this plant closes, Oregon will be coal-free. After negotiations with the Sierra Club, other environmental groups, union leaders, religious groups, public health advocates, and state officials, Washington State Governor Christine Gregoire announced that the local utility would close part of its huge power plant in Centralia in 2020 and the remainder in 2025. Bruce Nilles of the Sierra Club says, "This agreement is sending a message that states are getting serious about combating global warming pollution and are taking steps to open up markets for home-grown clean energy."

New York City Mayor Michael Bloomberg announced in July 2011 that he was contributing $50 million to the Beyond Coal campaign. Sierra Club head Michael Brune called this a "game changer." When Bloomberg, one of the most successful entrepreneurs of his generation, said coal has to go, it reverberated not only across the country but around the world.

One reason for the success of the Beyond Coal campaign is that Americans by and large simply do not like coal. A 2013 Gallup poll found that coal is Americans' least-favored energy source, far behind cleaner sources like wind and solar.

Although Beyond Coal is a national campaign, closures actually occur at the community level with the grassroots involvement of local groups, including health organizations alarmed by the effects of breathing coal plant emissions. Civil rights groups, concerned about the disproportionate impact of coal pollution on communities of color, also are involved. This combination of environmentalists, health advocates, and civil rights groups has created a formidable force in favor of replacing coal.

When the Sierra Club succeeds in closing a coal-fired power plant, it does not simply walk away from the site. Even while its members are working to close the plant, they also work with local communities to replace the coal-fired electricity with efficiency gains and clean electricity from wind, solar, or geothermal. In Los Angeles, for example, the local utility, the Sierra Club, and other organizations developed a plan to move off coal while protecting the pocketbooks of low-income residents. They celebrated a major victory in March 2013 when Mayor Antonio Villaraigosa announced that Los Angeles would go coal-free by 2025. The city will replace the dirty energy with energy efficiency and a massive urban rooftop solar initiative.

The Sierra Club has also launched a major challenge to coal on college and university campuses, and a broad cross-section of U.S. higher education institutions has become involved. The University of Illinois and Cornell University were among the first schools making coal-free commitments. At the University of North Carolina, another early adopter, Chancellor Holden Thorp announced in 2010 that the university was phasing out coal use. He remarked that "coal cars pulling up... to the plant is not particularly good symbolism for a university that teaches people about climate change and the frontiers of energy research." Even coal-state schools such as the University of Tennessee, Western Kentucky University, and the University of Louisville have pledged to end coal use on campus. By late 2014, a third of all on-campus coal plants in the United States had been retired or were slated to retire. These successes have encouraged the Sierra Student Coalition to broaden its campaign on fossil fuels and join forces with groups such as 350.org that are working to encourage schools to divest from coal, oil, and natural gas companies.

Investment banks are also taking a dim view of coal. Analysts at Goldman Sachs write: "We believe that thermal coal's current position atop the fuel mix for global power generation will be gradually eroded." They note that "most thermal coal growth projects will struggle to earn a positive return." There are three reasons for this. One, environmental regulations on coal use are becoming more stringent. Two, the competition from natural gas, solar, and wind is intensifying. And three, investment in energy efficiency gains will lead to less coal use. Kevin Parker, while serving as the global head of asset management at Germany's Deutsche Bank, put it this way: "Coal is a dead man walkin'.... Banks won't finance [coal-fired power plants]. Insurance companies won't insure them. The EPA is coming after them.... And the economics to make it clean don't work."

The mounting opposition to coal has led to shrinking or even disappearing profit margins, resulting in precipitous drops in the stock values of many coal-related companies. The Stowe Global Coal Index—a composite index of companies from around the world whose principal business involves coal—dropped 70 percent between April 2011 and September 2014, whereas the S&P 500 grew almost 50 percent during the same time.

Peabody Energy, the largest U.S. coal producer, is having a difficult time. Its market value dropped from roughly $10 billion in November 2006 to $3.9 billion in mid-September 2014, a decline of 61 percent. During the first half of 2014, Peabody's market value fell 17 percent even as the Dow Jones global energy index climbed 12 percent. Because of its lower market value, Peabody was removed from the S&P 500.

Arch Coal, the other leading U.S. coal company, saw its market value drop a stunning 94 percent from April 2011 to September 2014. It suffered heavily from the shrinking U.S. coal market and dwindling demand from China for steel-making coal.

While coal use is dropping fast in the United States, it is growing in the developing world. But this could slow down somewhat as financing becomes more difficult. In June 2013 President Obama announced that the United States would no longer use public money to finance coal plants internationally except in special circumstances. The World Bank followed suit the next month and announced that it too would no longer fund coal plants. And in July 2013 the European Investment Bank placed strict limits on lending for new or renovated coal plants. Only facilities with carbon emissions below a certain threshold will be eligible for funding. Ingrid Holmes of the U.K.-based environmental think tank E3G said this move "puts the bankers ahead of politicians in terms of tangible action."

Still, coal use worldwide is expanding. A number of countries are planning to build hundreds of new coal plants, including, importantly, India. But India is running into problems at the local level. Developing India's coal reserves threatens some of its remaining forests, ones that are protected because they are home to the country's surviving tiger population. Local communities are fighting back against planned coal plants that displace thousands of people. In one example, residents of coastal Sompeta teamed up with fishers, farmers, shepherds, doctors, women's groups, and labor groups to combat the construction of a massive 1,980-megawatt plant. Their peaceful opposition was met with violence, resulting in the deaths of two fishermen. The battle, which was also waged in Indian courts, ended when the coal plant lost its land allotment, effectively blocking its construction.

India's coal sector is also suffering from the recent "Coalgate" scandal, which brought to light some $33 billion in coal leases that were not sold by open bidding but were practically given away to large, politically connected companies and wealthy individuals. Newspapers jumped on this issue with scathing editorials. In late 2014 the Indian Supreme Court canceled over 200 coal leases granted between 1993 and 2010 that now must go through new auctions.

Coal India, a semi-government agency that is the world's largest coal miner, was expected to prosper or at least achieve a certain level of efficiency. But although it effectively has a monopoly, it frequently misses production goals. In late 2014 the government took the first steps toward opening up coal mining to private companies. The end of Coal India's monopoly may be in sight.

Taxes on coal mined in or imported to India have recently doubled, with the extra revenue going toward renewable energy, namely solar. Shortly after taking office in 2014, Prime Minister Narendra Modi announced that he would be pushing hard for solar expansion at the national level just as he had at the state level when he was chief minister of Gujarat. And even Coal India is installing solar panels on some of its facilities to cut costs.

At the same time, however, the Modi administration is calling for a doubling of domestic coal use by 2020 as it tries to bring electricity to those who do not yet have it. The potential for this much growth from the world's third largest coal user—and the third largest emitter of carbon dioxide—is worrisome. Indian cities already rival their Chinese counterparts for the world's worst air pollution. More coal plants would only make this situation worse, pushing India's estimated annual death toll from coal-related pollution to over 150,000.

China consumes more coal than the rest of the world combined. It gets some 80 percent of its electricity from the fossil fuel. However, China's annual growth in coal use has dropped from more than 10 percent in some years over the last decade to less than 4 percent in 2013. And in the first 11 months of 2014, coal use in China dropped for the first time in decades, which may mean that peak coal is here.

Several factors are behind China's coal slowdown. For one, rising public anger over pollutants from coal-fired power plants is damaging the coal prospect. The effect of pollution on the Chinese people has become such a pressing concern that the government can no longer ignore it. Another factor is water. Coal plants use large amounts of water for cooling. In the agriculturally productive North China Plain, where water tables are falling rapidly, the construction of more coal plants and their associated water needs will simply accelerate the drop in the water table until the aquifer is depleted. As water scarcity worsens, China will be facing a choice between using water to cool coal plants or using it for irrigation to produce rice and wheat. If it opts for the former, China will need to import even more grain than it does today, putting additional pressures on the world's exportable supplies and quite likely driving the world price of grain higher while at the same time raising the global thermostat.

In September 2013 Citi Research released a report entitled "The Unimaginable: Peak Coal in China." Looking at China's massive and unprecedented push to develop its abundance of wind resources and its recent catapult into a leading position in global solar panel installations, peak coal may no longer be so unimaginable. Besides the increased use of other energy sources and the challenges of air pollution, the report counts China's slowing economy and its energy efficiency improvements as reasons for a peak coming earlier than anticipated.

Some recent policy decisions will further decrease coal's prominence in China. Three provinces and three major cities have pledged to cut their coal use substantially by 2017. This includes major industrial centers such as Beijing, Heibei, and Shandong. Shandong, the leading provincial energy consumer, currently burns as much coal as Germany and Japan combined do. The use and sale of coal are banned in Beijing starting in 2020. And in November 2014 China and the United States announced a groundbreaking agreement to limit carbon dioxide emissions, which of course means limiting coal use. Soon after, China announced it would cap its coal use by 2020.

The Chinese government also recently imposed import tariffs of up to 6 percent on coal. Although China has large coal reserves of its own, it is also the world's leading importer, so its moves have a global effect. Indonesia and Australia, the two leading sources of China's coal imports, will both get tariff exemptions under free trade agreements. All countries sending coal to China need to meet stricter quality controls starting in 2015, as China is banning the use of high-sulfur coal in populous areas to help improve air quality.

China's coal imports from Australia have been on the rise. Australia's relationship with coal is an uneasy one. The country decreased its own coal use 20 percent since peaking in 2006, but its exports to countries including China, Japan, and South Korea are increasing. Despite coal's dimming future and its general unpopularity among citizens, Australian decisionmakers are doubling down on last century's fuel, moving forward with new mines and port expansions. Shortly after repealing the country's carbon tax in 2014, Australia's Prime Minister Tony Abbott opened a new coal mine with the declaration that "coal is good for humanity." Even though it is already operating below capacity, the major port at Newcastle is scheduled to expand to increase its ability to export coal. Whether the port will ever use the new capacity remains to be seen.

U.S. coal companies are also looking for markets abroad to replace shrinking domestic demand. Exports of coal to China, almost non-existent in 2007, have grown to 7.5 million tons of coal. The U.S. coal industry hopes that this grows quickly. Over much of the past decade, total U.S. coal exports climbed, reaching an all-time high of 114 million tons in 2012. Exports then fell in 2013 and 2014. The question now facing the U.S. coal industry is not just whether exports can grow but whether the current level can be sustained.

One of the world's largest coal reserves is located in the Powder River Basin of Wyoming and Montana. Until recently, U.S. coal companies had few options other than to use ports in Seattle and British Columbia to export that coal. But as the interest in moving coal through the Pacific Northwest grows, this region could find itself serving as the jumping-off point for close to 100 million tons of Asia-bound coal every year if proposed new terminals are built. Needless to say, handling this much coal in northwestern coastal ports, with all the associated coal dust, is of great concern to those who live there. In addition, the growing number of ships on the Columbia River and the added rail traffic could interfere with the local flow of transported goods.

Lined up in opposition to more coal exports are the Sierra Club, the Natural Resources Defense Council, and a number of other national and regional environmental and local citizens' groups. Also aligned with the environmental groups is the Lummi Nation, a Native American tribe that once inhabited much of the Pacific Northwest region, who are concerned about the threats to health and fisheries, as well as about preserving culturally important sites. Cesia Kearns, a Beyond Coal campaigner in the region, says: "Coal exports threaten our health and public safety. This has been garnering public outcry like I have not seen before. People are up in arms about it."

Governor John Kitzhaber of Oregon and almost 90 other elected officials have joined the EPA in asking for a comprehensive analysis of the effect of the proposed wholesale increase in coal shipments through the region. The situation is ironic. Oregon and Washington are being asked to serve as a conduit for global warming pollution in Asia, while at the same time they are closing their own coal-fired power plants to help prevent climate change from spiraling out of control.

In early January 2014, Oregon Public Broadcasting reported that Goldman Sachs was backing away from one of the proposed terminals. In pulling out of the project, Goldman Sachs drove another nail into the coal coffin. As the options for exporting through the Pacific Northwest close, companies are looking south to the Gulf of Mexico. But there they are finding local opposition for many of the same reasons, plus concerns over coastal restoration. Residents want a healthy coast to help protect them from the next hurricane. It is hard to find a community eager to support such a dirty fuel.

The world is waking up to the true casualties of burning coal: clean air, safe water for drinking and irrigating crops, and a relatively stable climate. These costs unmask "cheap coal." Many countries—including the United States and China, the world's two largest economies—have realized this and are beginning to move away from coal. As the transition to renewable energy accelerates, more coal will stay in the safest place for it: underground.

Data, endnotes, and additional resources can be found at Earth Policy Institute, www.earth-policy.org.

4

Nuclear Power in Decline

Nuclear power, once lauded as an energy source that would be "too cheap to meter," is becoming too costly to use. For the world as a whole, nuclear power generation peaked in 2006 and dropped by more than 10 percent by 2013. In the United States—the country with the most reactors—nuclear generation peaked in 2010, then dropped by nearly 3 percent by 2014. In second-place France, nuclear output has dropped nearly 7 percent since peaking in 2005. Similar declines can be seen in several other leading countries. These trends are likely to continue and even to accelerate as the world nuclear fleet ages and as solar- and wind-generated electricity comes online at a much lower cost than electricity from new nuclear plants.

The idea of using nuclear technology for peaceful purposes was brought to the fore with U.S. President Dwight D. Eisenhower's "Atoms for Peace" speech to the U.N. General Assembly in 1953. The 1960s and 1970s saw a boom in nuclear plant construction. Then new construction starts dropped sharply, and the worldwide growth in nuclear power generation slowed in the mid-1980s. As a share of global electricity generation, nuclear power reached nearly 18 percent in 1996. But by 2013, it accounted for less than 11 percent.

Industry analysts Mycle Schneider and Antony Froggatt write in their annual *World Nuclear Industry Status Report* that the number of operating reactors worldwide peaked at 438 in 2002. By July 2014, the total had dropped to 388 reactors operating in 31 countries—with most of the decline coming from the massive closure of plants in Japan following the 2011 Fukushima accident. Of the world's remaining reactors, exactly 100 were in the United States. France came next, with 58 nuclear reactors, followed by Russia with 33 and South Korea, China, India, and Canada each with around 20. The other countries rounding out the top 10 were the United Kingdom, Ukraine, and Sweden.

Typically, as more experience is gained with a power generation technology, costs decline. For example, with both wind and solar, costs have been dropping for years from both technological advances and economies of scale. But in one of the ironies of energy economics, the cost of nuclear power plants has increased over time.

A key contributor to rising costs is that plants are taking longer to build. For a number of reasons—including plant design changes, contract disputes, new safety regulations, and shortages of parts or labor—construction schedule delays are the rule, not the exception. For the 37 nuclear reactors that came online between 2004 and mid-2014, the average construction time was 10 years. China and India, which accounted for 20 of these 37 units, averaged 6 and 7 years respectively. But for Russia and Ukraine, construction times averaged 24 and 19 years respectively—nearly a human generation. Iran's first and only reactor took 36 years to build.

As of mid-2014, close to 70 reactors were still under construction worldwide. Mycle Schneider reports that

49 of them were behind schedule, including 20 of the 27 under construction in China. All nine of Russia's reactors were off schedule, as were the five being built in the United States. Even if all of these reactors are eventually completed, the additional generating capacity is unlikely to offset the capacity loss from retirements.

Construction on one of the U.S. reactors, Watts Bar 2 in Tennessee, began in 1972. The project, which was put on hold in the 1980s and revived in 2007, was scheduled to be completed in 2012 for a total of $2.5 billion. Then in early 2012 the utility building the reactor announced that the startup date would be moved to 2015 and the cost would rise to between $4 billion and $4.5 billion. If the plant is completed in 2015, it will have logged 43 years from start to finish—more time than it took to build the Panama Canal.

The other four U.S. nuclear units under construction, two each in Georgia and South Carolina, are the only projects still alive out of the dozens of new reactors planned in the 2000s as part of the "nuclear renaissance" touted by the industry. In June 2014, Georgia officials warned that the first new reactor at Plant Vogtle would be online in early 2018 instead of April 2016 as initially projected. The $14 billion price tag for the two reactors could rise by $2 million for every day of delay. And in August, an even longer delay was announced for the first new South Carolina reactor, tacking on an estimated $1 billion to the project's initial $10 billion cost. In each case, ratepayers are already paying for the projects, regardless of whether the plants are ever completed.

France, which gets more of its electricity from nuclear power than any other country—some 75 percent—has one remaining reactor under construction. Begun in 2007, the third unit at the Flamanville nuclear plant was projected to cost $4.5 billion and be finished in 2012.

Both targets were missed. Now the project may be finished in 2017 and cost at least $11.6 billion. A similar cost escalation has hit the lone reactor under construction in Finland, which broke ground in 2005. It will not go online until late 2018 at the earliest, nearly a decade later than originally planned.

One of the most staggering cases of cost escalation involves a project not yet under construction as of this writing. Beginning in 2005, the British government set its sights on a revival of U.K. nuclear power, promising 10 new reactors. These generators would be built for $3 billion each, need no subsidies, and start producing electricity in 2017. When European Union officials finally approved the plan in October 2014, however, it had been reduced to just two reactors, both heavily subsidized, with a start date of 2023. The U.K government will now cover roughly 70 percent of the estimated $39 billion it will cost French state-owned utility EDF to build the reactors. In addition, the government has agreed to pay EDF twice the current wholesale market rate for the electricity generated by the plant.

As plants age, operation and maintenance become more expensive. For the United States, which has some of the oldest nuclear power plants, this is a growing concern. Credit Suisse reports that the cost of operating aging U.S. reactors is rising 5 percent a year. Meanwhile, fuel costs are climbing 9 percent annually. These rising costs are not only discouraging the construction of new plants, they are leading to the closure of existing ones.

Four U.S. reactors were retired in 2013 because it did not make economic sense to continue operations. Southern California Edison decided to retire two reactors near San Diego rather than pay to repair a leak in a brand-new steam generator. Duke Energy shuttered a Florida nuclear unit because needed repairs were too costly and time-consuming. And Dominion Resources retired a Wisconsin reactor—recently approved by the U.S. Nuclear Regulatory Commission to extend operations until 2033—citing declining profits. A fifth reactor, Vermont Yankee, was shut down for good at the end of 2014, primarily because it was not cost-competitive.

Economist Mark Cooper of the Vermont Law School's Institute for Energy and the Environment has identified 37 more U.S. reactors that may be forced to close for economic reasons. With the operating costs of nuclear reactors escalating while the costs of solar and wind decline, the days for the remaining reactors are numbered.

This is not just a U.S. phenomenon. In 2012, EDF—the world's largest nuclear operator—logged a $2 billion income deficit largely because of rising costs. French data show the generating cost of nuclear there increased by one fifth from 2010 to 2013. In Germany, the giant utility E.ON will close an aging reactor seven months early in 2015 because operating costs exceed projected income. And three Swedish reactors are also having trouble as electricity sales lag costs.

In recent years, the major credit ratings agencies have tended to take a more negative view toward utilities with nuclear investments. One of those agencies, Moody's Investors Service, says companies building new nuclear plants put themselves at greater risk of a credit downgrade due in part to likely cost overruns and schedule delays, as well as vulnerability to being undercut by cheaper power options like wind and solar.

In general, European utilities heavy with nuclear plants have taken a beating in the market. Over the last seven years, EDF's share price has dropped by 70 percent. During the same period, the share price of Areva, the French government-owned company that is the world's largest builder of nuclear plants, dropped by 88 percent.

As the world fleet of nuclear plants—currently averaging more than 28 years in operation—ages, the question is whether to repair older plants or simply close them. It is not always clear exactly when a plant should be closed. As Matthew Wald notes in the *New York Times*, it is sometimes difficult for plant owners to distinguish between "middle-aged aches and pains" and "end-of-life crises."

Closing nuclear plants is costly. For the two California reactors retired in 2013, the 20-year decommissioning process will cost an estimated $4.4 billion. At the extreme end of decommissioning costs is the United Kingdom's Sellafield nuclear facility, site of the world's first commercial nuclear power plant. The U.K. government now estimates that decommissioning the four-reactor site, including cleaning up the legacy of weapons-grade plutonium that was produced in the 1950s, will cost a whopping $130 billion over the next century.

Disposal of nuclear wastes is yet another long-term cost—and an unsolved problem. As a result, nuclear waste is accumulating in every country that has nuclear power plants. As of 2014, the United States had nuclear waste stored at 80 temporary sites in 35 states. Nine states, among them California, Connecticut, and Illinois, have banned construction of new nuclear power plants until an acceptable means is developed to deal with the waste.

For more than 20 years the U.S. government said that the radioactive waste from the country's nuclear plants would be stored in Yucca Mountain, a proposed repository roughly 90 miles northwest of Las Vegas, Nevada. The projected cost to complete this repository, estimated at $58 billion in 2001, climbed to $96 billion by 2008. This comes to almost $1 billion per reactor—a staggering amount.

In addition to becoming more expensive, building the repository fell far behind schedule. Originally slated to start accepting waste in 1998, this was revised to 2017 and then again to 2020. But in 2009 the Department of Energy announced that the Yucca repository was being abandoned and that a search for a new site was under way. Although proponents have pushed to reanimate pursuit of the Yucca Mountain site, there is no guarantee this will happen. The U.S. nuclear industry appears to be caught in a trap it set for itself.

No country has come up with an acceptable long-term solution. South Korea, for example, has also accumulated large amounts of waste, 70 percent of it now in temporary storage pools. Park Jiyoung, a research fellow and nuclear scientist at the Asan Institute for Policy Studies, hit the nail on head when she said: "We cannot keep stacking waste while dragging our feet. If we fail to reach a conclusion [on how to manage spent fuel], it would be time to debate if we should stop nuclear power generation."

Some countries—namely France, India, Japan, Russia, and the United Kingdom—allow used nuclear fuel to be reprocessed, in which plutonium and uranium are separated from the other waste and later used again to fuel reactors. This does not solve the problems of waste storage and disposal because the volume of waste actually increases. Furthermore, isolating plutonium through waste reprocessing increases the risk that terrorists will obtain it for nuclear weapons or that countries with nuclear power facilities will develop their own weapons programs.

The global supply of experienced nuclear engineers and the availability of manufacturers to produce the parts for a nuclear power plant are both tightening. Older nuclear engineers are retiring, and young people are not entering the field—one that is widely perceived as dying— at a rate that will replace retirees. Skills and parts needed by the fading industry are not always readily available, causing costs to rise even more.

Nuclear power's overarching problem is that the economics do not work. But there is also always the risk of an accident—itself an enormous expense—as the world was reminded on March 11, 2011. At 2:46 pm that day, a magnitude 9.0 earthquake struck off Japan's northeast coast. Within one minute, more than 90 miles away, the three operating reactors at the six-unit Fukushima Dai-ichi nuclear power plant automatically shut down after detecting the tremors. The quake cut off grid power to the plant, prompting emergency diesel generators to start up. Unfortunately, the backup power system was destroyed when the earthquake spawned a massive tsunami, some 40 feet high, and floodwaters infiltrated the reactor buildings. Without electricity to maintain the flow of cooling water to the nuclear fuel rods, the reactor cores began overheating, cooling water evaporated, and the exposed nuclear fuel rods began to produce hydrogen gas.

That evening, the government declared a nuclear emergency and ordered evacuations within a 2-mile radius of the plant. By morning, the evacuation radius was increased to 6 miles. Following a hydrogen explosion at Unit 1 that afternoon, it was 12 miles.

Within four days of the earthquake and tsunami, all three previously operating reactors had melted down, releasing radioactive material and hydrogen. Explosions had rocked two more reactors, including Unit 4, which was off-line when disaster struck but where the spent fuel cooling system had been damaged. The world looked on in shock as 24-hour cable news channels covered this nuclear accident within the broader disaster that claimed some 15,900 lives.

The sheer scale of the recovery operation is difficult for anyone not directly involved with this work to envision. Nuclear industry analysts Schneider and Froggatt describe in detail some of the many dimensions of this effort. As of

May 2014, three years after the accident, 4,200 workers remained on-site. Recruiting workers to manage the site is becoming more difficult, for obvious reasons. It is taking 360 tons of water a day to continuously cool the molten fuel inside the plant's remains. As of July 2014, more than 500,000 tons of radioactive water were precariously stored on-site at the Fukushima plant. In trying to cope with the continuously growing quantity, plant operator TEPCO plans to expand the tank storage capacity there to hold 800,000 tons. Needless to say, with such a huge operation there have been many problems, including leaks of radioactive water into the soil, groundwater, and nearby Pacific Ocean. It has become a horror story without end.

The social effects of the Fukushima meltdown are extensive, to say the least. Some 130,000 people in Fukushima Prefecture have not been able to return to their homes. Another 137,000 evacuees from the earthquake- and tsunami-affected area are spread out over at least seven prefectures. Some 1,700 deaths, including suicides, are attributed to the disruptions and stresses caused by the meltdown.

It is estimated that decommissioning the Fukushima reactors may take 40 years and $100 billion. And this does not include decontamination of the surrounding area or the compensation that TEPCO is still paying to victims for lost property, mental suffering, and more—which combined may cost another $400 billion. Even more disturbing is the fact that this meltdown took place in one of the world's most technologically advanced societies.

This event altered the future of nuclear power. Prior to the Fukushima disaster, 16 of Japan's 54 reactors were already off-line for inspection or maintenance. When the earthquake and tsunami hit, more than a dozen reactors underwent emergency shutoffs, including the disabled

Fukushima Daiichi units. The rest of Japan's reactors eventually were taken off-line as well, either for inspection or because of earthquake vulnerability. Only two reactors subsequently restarted for any period of time, but these went off-line again in September 2013. The Fukushima experience has caused widespread public opposition to nuclear power in Japan. Most people do not want to restart any of the country's reactors. As of late 2014, no Japanese reactors were generating electricity. However, two reactors in Kagoshima Prefecture had met new safety requirements and gotten local approval to restart, setting up a possible early 2015 return to operation.

Immediately after the accident, attention in Japan turned to natural gas and oil as a substitute for the lost generating capacity. But with time there has also been rekindled interest in renewable sources of energy, such as solar, wind, and geothermal energy, each of which is widely available there. Although it is too early to tell for sure, Fukushima may have sounded the death knell for nuclear power in Japan.

Within days of the Fukushima accident, Chancellor Angela Merkel announced that Germany's oldest reactors would close. A plan to shut down all 17 of the country's nuclear reactors was agreed to in May 2011. The gap will be filled by harnessing Germany's green energy resources—primarily wind, solar, and geothermal energy.

Germany was not the only country to turn away from nuclear power. Switzerland, which was planning three new reactors, abandoned them. It also announced that its five reactors would close permanently when their operating licenses expired over the next couple of decades. Italy had been planning to restart its nuclear program, which had been halted in the 1980s, but in a June 2011 referendum, 90 percent of Italian voters chose to ban nuclear power. Belgium decided to phase out its seven nuclear reactors, which supply half of the country's electricity. France announced it would reduce its extreme dependence on nuclear power to 50 percent by 2025. Fukushima alerted the world to the potential dangers of nuclear power—concerns that had been largely set aside following two earlier accidents. On March 28, 1979, the Unit 2 reactor at the U.S. Three Mile Island nuclear generating complex suffered a partial meltdown. It began with either an electrical or a mechanical failure that compromised the plant's water-based cooling system. A series of operator errors followed, leading to overheating and a severe core meltdown. Although this was the most serious U.S. accident in the nuclear era, the radioactive releases were small and had no significant health effects on either workers at the plant or the community at large.

A 13-year cleanup program was devised after this accident, in the end costing close to $1 billion. While the human and environmental impact of the meltdown at the Three Mile Island facility appears to have been minimal, this should have been a wake-up call—a warning that accidents could happen at nuclear power plants, even in an industrial superpower.

Seven years later, in the early morning hours of April 26, 1986, the Unit 4 reactor at the Chernobyl nuclear generating plant in Ukraine, then part of the Soviet Union, exploded. Radioactive isotopes were blasted several miles into the atmosphere. Carried in all directions by the winds over the next 10 days, radioactive fallout contaminated 58,000 square miles of Ukraine, Belarus, and Russia and was detected at lower levels throughout the northern hemisphere. The effect of this explosion on the workers at the plant, the people who were most directly exposed to the radiation, was severe. Of the 134 workers who developed acute radiation sickness from high exposure, 28 died within three months. Thousands of children living in the area developed thyroid cancer.

The severe contamination in the 19-mile exclusion zone surrounding the plant made it uninhabitable. Nearly 200 villages were abandoned. The town of Pripyat, which had 45,000 residents and was within two miles of the Chernobyl plant, was immediately evacuated. It remains a ghost town. Although it has been nearly 30 years since the accident, the costly cleanup is still going on. With limited resources, the Ukrainian government has moved slowly. It may take another 100 years to finish the job.

Numerous studies have been undertaken to try to count the number of deaths from the Chernobyl nuclear fallout, including from the radioactive plumes that drifted over Europe, but the estimates range widely. Even harder to measure is the psychological toll that follows nuclear accidents on top of the physical and financial stresses. There is evidence that the stress of living in contaminated areas may have contributed to higher rates of alcoholism and smoking.

The total cost of dealing with the Chernobyl disaster thus far is difficult to estimate, but it could easily be in the hundreds of billions of dollars. As of the mid-2000s, Ukraine was still spending 5–7 percent of its national budget on Chernobyl-related programs and benefits.

The United States and some 30 other countries are financing a 32,000-ton arch to cover the aging "sarcophagus" that entombs the damaged Chernobyl reactor in order to contain radiation in case the sarcophagus collapses. It has a scheduled completion date of 2017.

It is clear that the risks posed by a catastrophic nuclear power accident are high. In the United States, the public is on the hook for most potential damages. In 1957 the U.S. Congress passed the Price-Anderson Act, which shelters U.S. utilities with nuclear power plants from the cost of an accident. Under the act, utilities are required to maintain private accident insurance of $375 million per reactor site. In the event of a catastrophic accident, every nuclear utility would be required to contribute up to $121 million for each of its licensed reactors to help cover the accident's cost.

The collective cap on nuclear operator liability for personal injury and property damage is $13 billion. So any accident costing more than that would have to be covered by taxpayers. Unfortunately, an estimate by the Sandia National Laboratories indicates that a worst-case accident could cost $700 billion.

Few of the cost calculations for nuclear power that are used by utilities are complete. If the full cost were included upfront, it would be impossible to justify building nuclear plants.

In stark contrast to nuclear power's darkening prospects, wind and solar power are surging ahead, as described in the following chapters. Global wind power generation has grown on average 26 percent a year over the last decade, while electricity from solar photovoltaics (PV) has grown 51 percent annually. During 2013, wind and solar PV together added 72,000 megawatts of generating capacity worldwide. Nuclear power, on the other hand, suffered a net loss of 1,500 megawatts.

In both China and India, wind farms generated more power in 2013 than nuclear plants did. Wind has not only overtaken nuclear power generation in China, it is in a steep upward climb. Nuclear power is continuing to expand there at 10 percent a year, but this is a much slower pace than the growth of wind. From 2008 to 2013, wind generation in China expanded a remarkable 59 percent a year.

And as France—for years the poster child for nuclear power—reduces its nuclear reliance over the next decade, it will boost renewable energy's share in its electricity mix from 16 percent to perhaps 40 percent. A big buildup of wind power, along with gains in energy efficiency and more solar power, will be key components of France's shift away from nuclear. It simply makes more sense to build new wind farms and solar arrays instead of new nuclear plants. Like nuclear power, wind and solar power generate electricity without climate-disrupting carbon emissions. But they do it more affordably and without the financial, environmental, and health risks associated with nuclear. Wind and solar installations come online in a fraction of the time that it takes to construct a nuclear plant. And once they do, the fuel is free, local, and unlimited.

The overall situation is that as of late 2014 some 31 countries were still operating nuclear power plants, but scarcely half as many were building new ones. Most of the planned build-out is in countries with centrally planned economies. But even in the absence of a free market, the high costs of nuclear power make it a poor energy choice. Nuclear power's best years are now history. The recent worldwide decline in nuclear generation is not a temporary dip but rather the beginning of the end of nuclear power.

Data, endnotes, and additional resources can be found at Earth Policy Institute, www.earth-policy.org.

5

The Solar Revolution

In April 1954, top scientists gathered in Washington, D.C., to hear something new: voice and music broadcast by a solar-powered radio transmitter. Scientists at Bell Labs in New Jersey were demonstrating their invention, the first practical solar cell, which was made of silicon. This breakthrough paved the way for the solar revolution taking place today on rooftops and in massive ground-mounted solar farms around the world.

Solar cells, also called solar photovoltaics or PV, powered U.S. satellites during the 1960s space race with the Soviet Union. But PV technology was still too expensive to be used for much else until the Arab oil embargo of 1973. Amid rising fears about energy security, governments and private firms poured billions of dollars into solar research and development, reaping big gains in efficiency and cost reductions. This led to widespread use of PV in the 1980s for powering telephone relay stations, highway call boxes, and similar applications.

Japanese and U.S. companies became early leaders in PV manufacturing for uses both large and small. For example, Japanese firms such as Sharp and Kyocera pioneered the use of solar cells in pocket calculators. A credit-card-sized solar-powered calculator from 1983 still helps us do quick calculations.

In the mid-1980s, Germany joined the United States and Japan in the race for PV production dominance, but by the early years of the new millennium, Japanese and U.S. companies accounted for roughly 70 percent of the world's PV output.

Forward-thinking energy policies in Germany were the catalyst that spurred solar power's astounding growth over the last decade or so. By guaranteeing renewable power producers access to the grid as well as a long-term premium price for their electricity, the German government's policy made going solar economically attractive. A reinvigorated German PV manufacturing industry climbed back into the number two spot behind Japan. As world production increased to meet demand, the price of solar panels dropped, helping to drive demand higher.

With demand for PV cells growing quickly, China—factory to the world—got into the game. Beginning around 2006, a boom in the Chinese PV industry massively expanded global production and drove prices down even further. Today China is a solar manufacturing giant, producing close to two thirds of the world's PV—more than the United States, Japan, and Germany combined.

The decline in PV panel prices over the decades is astonishing. In 1972, they cost over $74 per watt. The average price as of mid-2014 was less than 70¢ per watt—99 percent cheaper. (For reference, the typical U.S. rooftop system today has between 2 and 10 kilowatts of generating capacity. One kilowatt equals 1,000 watts.)

Around the world, solar installations are growing by leaps and bounds on residential and commercial rooftops and in solar farms, also called solar power plants or parks, that can cover thousands of acres. Between

2008 and 2013, as solar panel prices dropped by roughly two thirds, the PV installed worldwide skyrocketed from 16,000 to 139,000 megawatts. That is enough to power every home in Germany, a country with 83 million people. In its January 2014 solar outlook report, Deutsche Bank projected that 46,000 megawatts would be added to global PV capacity in 2014 and that new installations would jump to a record 56,000 megawatts in 2015. The International Energy Agency in Paris, which is typically conservative in its renewable energy forecasts, has been revising its solar projections upward. As recently as 2011 it forecast 112,000 megawatts of solar generating capacity by 2015—a figure the world left far behind in 2013. The organization now projects that by 2018 the total will be 326,000 megawatts of generating capacity, but the world will likely come close to this in 2016.

As solar power installations spread, it is worth remembering a point often made in the energy literature to convey the sheer scale of the solar resource: The sunlight striking the earth's surface in just one hour delivers enough energy to power the world economy for one year.

The largest solar power projects in the world just five years ago seem small by today's standards. An 80-megawatt PV park in Canada was the largest when it was finished in 2010. Now there are utility-scale solar power plants being built with hundreds of megawatts of generating capacity. A planned Japanese project on a small island near Nagasaki will have a 430-megawatt capacity, for instance. In California, it is not unusual today to see solar power plants being built with 300–500 megawatts of generating capacity.

Deutsche Bank notes that as of early 2014, solar PV was already competitive with average residential, commercial, or industrial electricity rates in 14 countries and in California, even without subsidies. For example, residential rooftop solar came in 25 percent cheaper than grid electricity in both California and South Africa—and at less than half the cost of power from the grid in Chile. In Italy, where PV systems now generate nearly 8 percent of electricity, solar was some two thirds cheaper than the grid average in both the residential and the industrial market.

Solar power also beats the average grid cost of electricity for the German residential and industrial markets. Germany is no tropical paradise. Indeed, its solar resource resembles that of rainy Seattle, Washington. But the government's policy commitment to renewable energy allowed Germany to become number one in installed PV capacity in 2005, a position it still held at the start of 2014. Some 1.4 million solar systems with a combined generating capacity of 36,000 megawatts, more than one quarter of world capacity, had been installed in Germany by then. Roughly 5 percent of the country's electricity was generated by solar panels in 2013. In the first 11 months of 2014, Germany's solar share rose to nearly 7 percent.

But solar power is about to have a new capacity leader. Annual installations in Germany and in Europe more broadly have slowed in recent years as incentives were reduced. Now China, which was slow getting started with PV installations, is going full-speed ahead. By more than doubling its PV generating capacity to 18,300 megawatts in 2013, China ousted Italy from the second place position. With planned 2014 installations adding up to 13,000 megawatts of new solar generating capacity, China is positioned to soon lead the world in capturing energy from the sun.

As governments see how quickly solar power can be installed, they may realize that their official capacity targets are too modest. China's initial goal for 2020 was to have 20,000 megawatts in operation. This was then raised to 50,000 megawatts, but in May 2014 China stunned the world by announcing a new, even more ambitious goal: 70,000 megawatts by 2017.

In Australia, a major coal producer and exporter, coal accounts for roughly two thirds of electricity generation. Solar power is gaining importance in the energy mix, however, as PV prices fall and rooftop solar systems spread. By the beginning of 2014, one out of every seven Australian homes was using rooftop solar PV for electricity. In 2007 there were only 8,000 rooftop solar systems in Australia. Now there are over a million.

Part of the attraction for Australians in going solar is that residential electricity prices have soared. Beginning in 2009, power transmission and distribution companies spent some $45 billion (Australian) updating and expanding the electricity network in this spread-out country. Perhaps half of that money was spent to meet an anticipated surge in demand that never came, in part due to more people generating some of their own electricity with rooftop PV.

Largely because of this infrastructure overinvestment, customers are now paying twice as much for electricity from the grid as before. Australian energy journalist Giles Parkinson reported in July 2014 that residential solar costs range from 12¢ to 18¢ (Australian) per kilowatt-hour (kWh) and may soon drop below 10¢ per kWh. Meanwhile, monthly transmission and distribution charges alone come to 15¢ per kWh—that's more than half the average bill. The bottom line is that in a growing number of places in Australia, coal-fired power would not be able to compete with solar even if the coal itself were free.

In Japan, the adoption of solar technology in both residential and nonresidential sectors accelerated sharply following the Fukushima nuclear power disaster, due largely to generous government solar incentives introduced after the accident. During 2013, Japan added nearly 7,000 megawatts of solar PV, doubling its installed PV generating capacity to 14,000 megawatts. This brought Japan halfway to its national solar goal for 2020. Some Japanese home builders are promoting solar houses to gain a competitive sales edge over other builders. Ichijo Co., a leading home builder, reported for example that 90 percent of the houses it sold in 2012 were equipped with solar panels.

Another sleeping giant, India, is waking up to its solar potential. By the start of 2014 it had 2,300 megawatts of PV generating capacity in operation, most of it in the sun-rich northwest desert states of Gujarat and Rajasthan. The official Indian goal, as set in 2010 by the National Solar Mission, is to have 22,000 megawatts of solar generating capacity in operation by 2022. In late 2014, India's energy minister stated that the government intends to boost the solar target to a startling 100,000 megawatts by 2022.

In December 2014 India's government approved a plan to facilitate the development of 25 "ultra-mega" solar parks of at least 500 megawatts each by 2019. State governments will choose developers and identify land for proposed projects, then apply to the federal Ministry of New and Renewable Energy for project approval. All told, the government aims to install some 20,000 megawatts of utility-scale PV in these parks. The 590-megawatt Charanka solar park in Gujarat—of which nearly 40 percent is now online—may be used as a model.

India's solar development will be partly funded by the recently doubled tax on coal mined domestically or imported into the country. This is a revenue transfer that simultaneously discourages the use of coal and provides investment capital for solar generation.

Another ambitious national solar goal comes from Saudi Arabia, where there are plans to develop some 41,000 megawatts of solar power by 2032. This will consist of 16,000 megawatts of power from solar PV and 25,000 megawatts from concentrating solar thermal power (a technology discussed in more detail later in this chapter). If these plants were in service today, they could supply up to two thirds of Saudi Arabia's electricity.

There is no national solar power capacity target in the United States, but PV is finally surging in the country that invented it. U.S. PV generating capacity jumped by a record 4,700 megawatts in 2013 to reach 12,000 megawatts overall, a growth of 65 percent. The market analysts at GTM Research projected another 6,500 megawatts would be added to U.S. solar capacity in 2014.

At the state level, California has long been the leader in developing solar energy resources. Other high-ranking states, in order of installed capacity, are Arizona, New Jersey, North Carolina, Massachusetts, and Nevada. This list shows, as we learned with Germany, that local solar intensity is only one of the influences on solar power development. Policy also plays a key role. New Jersey and Massachusetts, not especially sunny compared with the western states, have encouraged solar power through rebates for panel owners, renewable electricity mandates for utilities, and other policies. Contrast this with Florida, nicknamed "The Sunshine State." Policies that discourage PV adoption there have ensured that the state does not even appear on the top 10 list for total capacity.

Installing solar PV in the United States keeps getting more affordable. Between 2012 and 2013, U.S. residential rooftop PV system prices dropped 9 percent. For nonresidential systems, prices fell 16 percent. Prices continued falling in 2014. The overall price of PV system installations now depends much less on the price of the panels and much more on other facets of the business, including the costs of labor, other equipment, and landing customers.

Recent studies of solar power in California and Connecticut indicate that signing up new customers should get easier—and therefore cheaper—because adopting solar power can be contagious. One author, Kenneth Gillingham at Yale, says, "We find that if a neighbor close to you installs solar, you're much more likely to install than if a neighbor four miles away [does]."

By late 2014 there were nearly 600,000 individual PV systems in the United States, almost twice as many as in 2012. This number may well pass 1 million in 2016.

Increasingly, U.S. residential rooftop installations are owned by someone other than the property owner. In these arrangements, the installer puts up and maintains the PV system and the customer either pays a long-term fixed rate for the electricity generated or leases the system itself. Both models eliminate major up-front expenditures for consumers. According to GTM Research, in 2013 two thirds of all U.S rooftop installations fell into these camps, up from just over 40 percent in 2011. As PV systems become ever more affordable, however, the market is beginning to shift back to direct ownership, with customers aided by solar-specific loans.

Solar power's rapidly improving economics are leading to a solarization of the U.S. housing sector. In 2013, just 12 percent of U.S. homebuilders offered solar panels as an option for new single-family homes. More than half of them anticipate doing so by 2016. For multifamily homes, two thirds of builders will offer solar systems by 2016, up from 45 percent in 2013.

Four of the top five U.S. home construction firms— D.R. Horton, Lennar Corp., PulteGroup, and KB Home— now automatically include solar panels on every new house in certain markets, and they are rapidly expanding the practice as solar costs fall. In 100 of its subdivisions in California, for example, Lennar has included solar panels as standard. Soon the firm will do the same in developments in Colorado and several other states. Anyone buying one of these homes will be in the energy business.

Those for whom on-site solar power may not be a possibility—such as renters, condominium owners, or homeowners without the right rooftop conditions—can take advantage of the growing number of "community solar" options, where multiple participants have a stake in a shared PV project. The project may be owned by a utility or non-profit or by a new business venture formed by the community members themselves.

The rapid growth in private solar installations is leading to predictions of a "utility death spiral" in competitive electricity markets. As more customers in a utility's service area generate some of their electricity with rooftop PV, the utility loses money because it is selling those customers less of its product. And because PV generation displaces more expensive conventional electricity on the grid, it helps drive down power prices. This problem is especially acute in the midday hours when solar generation is strong and demand tends to be high, eroding the utility's formerly high peak-hour profits.

Even as it pulls in less money, the utility still has to run its plants and maintain its infrastructure, so it is then forced to raise its rates. This, along with the continued decline in solar system prices, encourages even faster growth in rooftop installations. Many utilities, with their old business model becoming obsolete, see distributed solar power as an existential threat. The question is whether to fight it or to adapt.

In Germany, impressive rooftop solar growth has helped put leading utilities on the ropes. It also has led to some fascinating developments as they try to reinvent themselves to survive in the new energy economy. The two largest German utilities, E.ON and RWE, each saw their market value drop by more than half between 2009 and 2013. The massive expansion of PV and wind power—another fuel-free source with low costs of operation—together with weak power demand drastically reduced their income and made their centralized power plants uneconomic to run. Indeed, RWE chief of strategy Thomas Birr said, "At the current market price, it is virtually impossible to operate conventional power stations economically...20 percent to 30 percent of our power stations currently cannot even cover their operating costs."

As a result, E.ON and RWE are in the process of shutting down or idling 19,000 megawatts of coal and natural gas plants. And both firms are now required to quickly shut down their nuclear plants to comply with Germany's plan to phase out nuclear by 2022. RWE posted a $3.8 billion loss in 2013—its first since 1949—and E.ON took a $5.6 billion loss in 2014.

Faced with an unsustainable status quo, these energy giants are moving to adapt. RWE will become more of an energy services company, managing and integrating solar and other renewables on the grid, consulting on energy efficiency with homeowners and businesses, and selling energy-saving tools such as smart thermostats.

In late 2014, E.ON announced it was splitting off the centralized power generation part of its business into a new company. When the split is finalized in 2016, E.ON will then focus on renewables, efficiency, and the pairing of rooftop PV with battery storage—an even more disruptive technology because it would allow customers to more easily disconnect from the grid completely.

Of course, many utilities worried about what growing solar PV generation means for their business are fighting back. One way that U.S. utilities are doing so is by attacking the net metering policies that now exist in 43 states. Under such a policy, when a utility customer's rooftop generation exceeds the household's needs, the surplus electricity is fed into the grid. The customer is credited for this excess electricity.

In late 2013, an Arizona utility became the first to gain traction against net metering. Arizona Public Service (APS), which says PV systems are being installed at a rate of more than 15 per day in the state, wanted customers with rooftop PV to pay a surcharge of up to $100 per month. After APS spent almost $4 million on ads in support of the proposal, regulators agreed to a much smaller surcharge, averaging $5 per month. By late 2014, measures to weaken or eliminate net metering policies had been proposed in at least 20 states. Some of these proposals were actually drafted by the American Legislative Exchange Council, a conservative political group whose members include representatives from the utility and fossil fuel industries.

Utilities trying to stifle solar power may soon realize that the effort is futile. The U.K.-based financial services firm Barclays downgraded the entire U.S. electricity sector in 2014, in part because in its view U.S. utilities are generally unprepared for the challenges posed by distributed solar power and battery storage. As Barclays analysts wrote, "whatever roadblocks utilities try to toss up... it's already too late."

The falling costs of solar-generated electricity are driving developments in the power sector at a pace that could not have been imagined even a few years ago. For example, in May 2014, Austin Energy, a publicly owned utility in Texas, signed a 150-megawatt power purchase agreement (a long-term contract to purchase electricity for a fixed price) with solar developer Recurrent Energy for just under 5¢ per kWh. Thus the electricity produced by this PV installation, which will be the largest in Texas when completed in 2016, greatly undercuts the local utility's natural gas–generated electricity at 7¢, its coal-fired power at 10¢, and its nuclear power at 13¢. Austin Energy is planning to get 55 percent of its electricity from renewable sources by 2025, up from 23 percent in mid-2014.

Betsy Engelking, a vice president at Minnesota-based wind and solar power developer Geronimo Energy, says that the price of solar power has fallen "about five years faster than anyone expected it to." To say that the fast-improving economics of solar power is attracting attention is an understatement. Major investors, including Warren Buffett and Ted Turner, are plowing billions of dollars into solar power plants.

In January 2013, for example, Buffett gave solar energy a huge financial boost when his MidAmerican Energy Holdings Company announced an investment of up to $2.5 billion in California in what is now known as the Solar Star project. At 580 megawatts, it will become the world's largest PV project when complete in late 2015. MidAmerican had earlier bought the Topaz solar farm in California, now the world's largest at 550 megawatts. As of its completion in late 2014, Topaz can generate enough electricity to power 180,000 California homes. MidAmerican also took a 49 percent stake in the 290-megawatt Agua Caliente plant in Arizona.

Both Topaz and Agua Caliente use thin-film PV, made of a cadmium-telluride compound, rather than the traditional silicon-based PV. The supplier, First Solar, the world's leading thin-film maker, is a U.S. company that does most of its manufacturing in Malaysia.

Ted Turner has teamed up with Southern Power, a utility serving eight states from California to North Carolina, to acquire seven solar plants approaching a combined 300 megawatts. The largest is a 140-megawatt solar park in Imperial County, California—another project using thin-film PV from First Solar—that began operating in October 2013.

Although photovoltaics are by far the most common way to convert the sun's energy into electricity, another approach is concentrating solar power (CSP), which uses mirrors to concentrate sunlight to drive conventional steam turbines or engines. The most prevalent CSP technology uses many rows of curved mirrors—"parabolic troughs"—to focus sunlight on fluid-filled tubes running the length of the troughs. The super-heated fluid then drives a steam turbine to generate electricity. Another kind of CSP is the "power tower," where a field of computer-operated mirrors concentrates sunlight on a central receiver to drive a steam turbine.

CSP generating capacity worldwide reached 4,100 megawatts in mid-2014. Spain and the United States totally dominate this source of electricity. Spain has dozens of small CSP plants, totaling 2,300 megawatts of capacity. The United States has more than 20 CSP plants, adding up to 1,500 megawatts, mostly in California and Arizona—both states with a high solar intensity.

One of the newer CSP facilities is the Solana plant in Arizona, a 280-megawatt parabolic trough plant. Ivanpah in California is the world's largest CSP plant, a power tower system with 390 megawatts of generating capacity. One of its attractions is that it can store up to six hours worth of heat energy in molten salts, enabling it to generate power long after sundown. Other recent additions to global capacity include the 100-megawatt Shams 1 plant in the United Arab Emirates; a 50-megawatt plant in Rajasthan, India; and the 10-megawatt first phase of a 50-megawatt plant being built in China's Qinghai Province.

In mid-2014 in Chile's Atacama Desert—known as the driest place on earth—the Spanish firm Abengoa began construction on a 110-megawatt CSP plant, a power tower with an impressive 18 hours of thermal energy storage in molten salts. If successful, this plant will be able to generate electricity around the clock. Despite its remarkable promise for energy storage, CSP's ambition to become a prominent global energy source has faded somewhat in recent years as the cost of photovoltaics has fallen much faster. As a result, several prospective CSP projects in the United States have been cancelled or replaced by PV. CSP costs still are falling, however, dropping by one third between 2010 and 2013 to reach 13¢ per kWh. The U.S. Department of Energy's SunShot program has set a goal of helping CSP to be fully cost-competitive at 6¢ per kWh by 2020. By that year, global CSP capacity is expected to reach 11,000 megawatts, but it could be much higher if SunShot reaches its mark.

Most people around the world rely on electricity from large power sources, transmitted via an electric grid. For the roughly 1.3 billion people in the world living in communities not yet connected, it is now often cheaper and more efficient simply to install PV panels rooftop-by-rooftop than to build a central power plant and transmission infrastructure. India and Bangladesh provide some inspiring examples of how rural residents in developing countries are bypassing the grid.

Millions of rural Indians rely on highly polluting, poorly illuminating, and increasingly costly kerosene lamps for home lighting. Solar power offers a solution. SELCO Solar, an independent offshoot of the Washington, D.C.-based Solar Electric Light Fund, has installed roughly 200,000 solar home lighting systems in rural India since its launch in 1995. According to SELCO's

Surabhi Rajagopal, a typical system that replaces two kerosene lamps with compact fluorescent bulbs or LEDs and can charge a mobile phone costs roughly $200. This includes the cost of installation and one year of maintenance. Because households spend roughly $60 annually on kerosene and mobile charging, a new solar home system pays for itself in a little over three years. SELCO works with regional rural banks to set up a workable loan for the customer, with monthly payments lower than what lighting and phone charging used to cost. Nationally, India's official goal is to replace kerosene lamps with 20 million solar lighting systems, potentially reaching 100 million people.

Switching from kerosene lamps to solar cells is particularly helpful in fighting climate change. Although the estimated 1.5 billion kerosene lamps used worldwide provide less than 1 percent of all residential lighting, they account for 29 percent of the lighting sector's carbon dioxide emissions. Kerosene lamps burn the equivalent of 1.3 million barrels of oil per day, equal to roughly half the daily oil production of Kuwait. With the price of kerosene rising and the cost of solar cells declining, the decision to make the switch becomes progressively easier.

A similar argument can be made for the economic and climate advantages of electricity from rooftop solar installations over the far costlier electricity from diesel generators. According to the solar consultancy Bridge to India, solar generation in India costs about one third to one half as much as diesel generation. Whether used for lighting homes or pumping water, solar electricity has a strong advantage.

Solar electricity generating technology is also benefiting millions of people in Bangladesh who might never have access to power from the grid. World Bank–led efforts since 2002 have helped install 3 million solar home systems. As of 2014, over 70,000 solar home systems were being installed every month. The World Bank's head person in Bangladesh, Christine E. Kimes, notes: "This is a proven model that works. Investing in electricity in rural areas empowers both men and women, leading to increased income and growth opportunities and reducing poverty."

When a villager buys a solar PV system, that person is buying a reliable, long-term supply of electricity. With no fuel costs and minimal maintenance needs, only the up-front outlay requires financing.

Another small-scale way to meet household energy needs with the sun is by using rooftop solar thermal collectors to heat water. China now has an estimated 2.8 billion square feet of rooftop solar water heaters installed, enough to supply 170 million Chinese households with hot water. This low-cost technology has leapfrogged into villages that do not yet have electricity. For roughly $300, villagers can install a rooftop solar collector and take their first hot showers.

In Europe, where energy costs are high, rooftop solar water heaters are also quite popular. In Austria, 15 percent of all households rely on them for hot water. Indeed, in some Austrian villages nearly all homes have rooftop collectors. Germany is also forging ahead. An estimated 2 million German homes are now relying on rooftop solar systems for water heating. Some 40 percent of these systems in Austria and Germany are combination systems, heating space as well as water.

Brazil is Latin America's leader in solar water heating, in part because of programs that require solar hot water systems in new housing for the very poor. The state of Hawaii in the United States has its own mandate, which took effect in 2010, stipulating that all new single-family home construction must include solar water heaters.

Solar hot water systems have taken hold in parts of the eastern Mediterranean too, where the island nation of Cyprus leads the world in rooftop solar collectors per person. And some 85 percent of Israeli households use their rooftops for water heating.

From the rooftops of homes, schools, businesses, and government buildings to sports stadiums, parking lots, former landfills, and deserts, a solar energy revolution is unfolding. The rapidly increasing competitiveness of PV in particular suggests that solar energy has an even more promising future than many analysts have expected. For much of humanity, it heralds cheaper electricity. But for many of the world's low-income residents, it means electricity in their homes for the very first time.

Data, endnotes, and additional resources can be found at Earth Policy Institute, www.earth-policy.org.

6

The Age of Wind

In the global transition from fossil fuels to wind and solar energy, wind has taken the early lead. Wind is abundant, carbon-free, and inexhaustible. It uses no water, no fuel, and little land. It also scales up easily and can be brought online quickly. Little wonder that wind power is expanding so fast.

Over the past decade, world wind power capacity grew more than 20 percent a year, its increase driven by its many attractive features, by public policies supporting its expansion, and by falling costs. By early 2014, global wind generating capacity totaled 318,000 megawatts, enough to power more than 80 million U.S. homes. Wind currently has a big lead on solar PV, which has enough worldwide capacity to power more than 20 million U.S. homes.

The leaders in wind generating capacity are China and the United States. At the start of 2014, China had 91,000 megawatts of wind generating capacity, followed by the United States with 61,000 megawatts. Germany ranked third, with 34,000 megawatts, followed by Spain and India with around 20,000 megawatts each. The

United Kingdom, Italy, France, and Canada were clustered together in the 8,000–10,000 megawatt range. With some impressive wind power achievements in several countries, it is becoming easier to visualize the new energy economy. In 2013, wind farms generated 34 percent of Denmark's electricity. Portugal's wind share was 25 percent. Spain and Ireland came in at around one fifth each. In fact, Spain's wind farms overtook coal plants as that country's number two electricity source in 2013 and narrowly missed overtaking nuclear power for the lead.

Within Germany, four states in the north are leading the world into the wind century: Mecklenburg-Vorpommern gets 65 percent of its electricity from wind, Schleswig-Holstein gets 53 percent, and Sachsen-Anhalt and Brandenburg each get 51 percent. Each of these states has passed the halfway mark in the transition to the new energy economy.

The year 2013 ended with a bang for wind energy in Europe. In the United Kingdom, strong winds in late November 2013 greatly boosted wind generation and allowed utilities to power down 7,900 megawatts of high-cost gas-fired generators, dramatically cutting their gas expenditures. Wind power met 13 percent of U.K. electricity needs during the week before Christmas. For the year, wind farms generated close to 8 percent of all U.K. electricity.

In December 2013, wind supplied 28 percent of Ireland's electricity. At times during the year, wind was responsible for half of the country's electricity. Denmark, however, won the wind sweepstakes: wind supplied 55 percent of its electricity during December. The next month, Denmark broke its own record, getting an incredible 62 percent of its electricity from wind.

Denmark—a country of fewer than 6 million people that is about one third the size of New York State—

embarked on its path toward such impressive wind generation as a result of the 1970s oil crises. Realizing that being more than 90 percent dependent on oil to satisfy its energy needs was no longer viable, Denmark initially turned to coal and to the prospect of building nuclear power plants. (Anti-nuclear public sentiment led to the abandonment of the latter idea.) The Danish government also used electricity taxes to fund research and development of renewable energy, helping nurture a fledgling wind power industry. The Danish wind company Vestas, which installed its first turbine in 1979, was the leading installer worldwide in 2013.

Wind turbine orders in the early 1980s from California—also spooked by the unpredictability of oil markets—were key in getting Denmark's wind industry going. Now, after nearly 40 years of Danish policies promoting renewable energy—including environmental taxation favoring efficiency and renewables over polluting energy sources—Denmark is well on its way to meeting a goal it set in 2012: getting 50 percent of its electricity from wind by 2020. Energinet.dk, Denmark's state-owned grid operator, reports that the share reached 39 percent in 2014.

Countries are adding wind power to their energy mix for a host of reasons. One of wind's attractions is its small footprint. Although a wind farm can cover many square miles, turbines occupy little land. Coupled with access roads and other permanent features, a wind farm's footprint typically comes to just over 1 percent of the total land area covered by the project.

Wind energy yield per acre is off the charts. For example, a farmer in northern Iowa could plant an acre in corn that would yield enough grain to produce roughly $1,000 worth of fuel-grade ethanol per year, or the farmer could put on that same acre a turbine that generates $300,000 worth of electricity per year. Farmers typically receive

$3,000 to $10,000 per turbine each year in royalties. The Iowa Wind Energy Association estimates that landowners in Iowa already collectively earn more than $12 million a year by hosting wind turbines.

In more densely populated areas, there is often local opposition to wind power—the NIMBY ("not in my backyard") response. But in the vast ranching and farming regions of the United States, wind is immensely popular for economic reasons. For ranchers in the Great Plains, farmers in the Midwest, or dairy farmers in upstate New York, there is a PIMBY—"put it in my backyard"—reaction. Rural communities compete with each other for wind farm investments and the additional tax revenue they bring that can be used to support schools and maintain roads.

Because turbines occupy such a small area of the land covered by a wind farm, ranchers and farmers can, in effect, double-crop their land, simultaneously harvesting electricity while grazing cattle or growing wheat or corn. As wind farms spread across the U.S. Great Plains, wind royalties for many ranchers will exceed their earnings from cattle sales.

In addition to being land-efficient, wind is also abundant. In the United States, three wind-rich states—North Dakota, Kansas, and Texas—have enough harnessable wind energy to collectively satisfy national electricity needs. A 2009 paper in the *Proceedings of the National Academy of Sciences* indicated that at the global level, on-shore wind farms could supply 40 times the electricity the world uses each year, or five times world energy needs. Wind is also not depletable. In contrast with fossil fuels, the amount of wind energy used today has no effect on the amount available tomorrow.

Wind's abundance is matched by its popularity. A January 2014 poll taken in Kansas, for example, showed that 76 percent of voters strongly support the harnessing of wind energy. And a national poll taken in the fall of 2013 by Navigant Research found that 72 percent of Americans are in favor of wind power. In the European Union, 89 percent of respondents in a 2011 poll were supportive.

Unlike fossil fuel and nuclear power plants, wind farms do not require water for cooling. As wind replaces coal and nuclear plants in power generation, it frees up water for irrigation, residential needs, and environmental purposes. And because it does not emit any airborne pollutants, it reduces the incidence of asthma and lung cancer. In contrast to coal plants, wind farms do not pollute water.

One of wind's strongest attractions is its low cost. With wind there are no fuel bills, so once a wind farm is completed, the only costs are those for operation and maintenance. This is a big reason why wind farm developers can sign long-term electricity supply contracts (power purchase agreements or PPAs) with utilities and private businesses at low fixed rates.

In the midwestern United States, for example, contracts are being signed at a price of 2.5¢ per kilowatt-hour (kWh), which compares with the nationwide average grid price of 10–12¢ per kWh. This price does reflect an important federal tax credit for wind farms, but Stephen Byrd of Morgan Stanley notes that even without the benefit of the tax credit, "some of these wind projects have a lower all-in cost than gas." Further, he says, "in the Midwest it's fairly vicious competition between very efficient wind farms—which are always called on first because they have no variable cost—and coal and nuclear." As the average PPA price for U.S. wind power keeps falling, natural gas, coal, and nuclear power plants will have an even harder time keeping up.

Wind power also has an advantage over conventional sources when it comes to construction time. While it may take a decade or more to build a nuclear power plant, for example, the construction time for the typical wind farm is one year or less.

One of the obvious downsides of wind is its variability. But as wind farms multiply, this becomes less of an issue. Because no two wind farms have identical wind profiles, each one added to a grid reduces variability. A Stanford University research team points out that if thousands of wind farms spread across the United States were connected by a national grid, wind would become a remarkably stable source of electricity.

Another point often raised in opposition to wind power is that birds are killed by the turbines' spinning blades. While bird deaths at wind farms are certainly a concern, improvements have been made over the years in turbine design, with blades turning much more slowly than in earlier models. Avoiding migratory pathways when siting wind farms has also become common practice. In comparison to the old energy economy's power priorities—like coal or nuclear power plants—wind farms cause far fewer avian deaths for each unit of electricity generated. At a broader level, bird deaths from wind farms are but a small fraction of those caused by collisions with buildings, power lines, and automobiles or by house cats.

As the modern wind industry began to take shape in the 1980s, the United States and Denmark dominated the world in wind power capacity. (The former held a healthy lead over the latter.) Then in the 1990s, India and countries in Europe—principally Germany, but also Spain, the United Kingdom, Italy, and France—threw their hats into the ring. By 1997, Germany had wrested the world wind power lead from the United States.

Ten years later, the United States reclaimed the title, but only held it for a few brief years because of what was happening in China. A law was passed there in 2005 to promote renewable energy development, setting the stage for exponential growth in wind power. Each year from 2006 to 2009, China's wind generating capacity doubled, and in 2010 it overtook the United States to become the world wind leader.

In 2013, China's wind farms generated more electricity than its nuclear power plants did. The gap likely widened further in 2014. Wind is now the country's third leading electricity source, behind coal and hydropower. Data from Harvard researchers, writing in the *Proceedings of the National Academy of Sciences*, indicate that China has enough harnessable wind energy to expand its total electricity consumption 10-fold.

In 2008, China's National Energy Administration selected several wind-rich northern provinces to host wind farm mega-complexes, each with at least 10,000 megawatts of generating capacity. These planned "Wind Bases," unprecedented in size, were intended to reach more than 100,000 megawatts of combined capacity by 2020.

The Chinese government, concerned about the underdeveloped electric grid in these remote locations and about project quality suffering with such rapid construction, has since scaled back the Wind Base plans. But even the more modest numbers are impressive. The 3,800-megawatt first phase of Gansu Province's Wind Base in Jiuquan is complete, with another 3,000 megawatts under construction in the second phase. In Hebei Province's Wind Base, some 1,400 megawatts of wind power is now operational, and nearly twice that much is in the construction stage.

Altogether, the Wind Base capacity either finished or under construction in Gansu, Hebei, Inner Mongolia, and Xinjiang Provinces comes to 19,000 megawatts.

With further wind farms planned and under construction, China should have little trouble meeting its official 2020 wind power goal of 200,000 megawatts. For perspective, that would be enough to satisfy the annual electricity needs of Brazil. Although China has the most installed wind power capacity, the United States produces more electricity from its wind farms than China or any other country does. This is primarily because China's wind farm construction has outpaced transmission and grid upgrades, forcing many turbines in remote regions to sit idle. Additionally, tax incentives for wind projects in China benefit project build-outs, whereas in the United States they reward actual electricity production.

Across the United States, there were 905 utility-scale wind farms in 39 states at the start of 2014, according to the American Wind Energy Association. They provided over 4 percent of the country's electricity generation during 2013, enough to power the equivalent of 15 million American homes.

Texas, California, Iowa, Illinois, and Oregon are the top five states in total installed wind generating capacity. Texas, long the U.S. leader in oil production, now also leads in wind, with 12,400 megawatts of capacity at the start of 2014. In California, the vanguard of wind power development, the capacity figure is 5,800 megawatts. If Texas and California were countries, they would rank in the top dozen wind power nations.

Tri Global Energy, a Dallas-based firm, has leased 640,000 acres in the Texas Panhandle, where it plans to build 16 wind farms. When completed within the next decade, these farms will have 6,600 megawatts of generating capacity, enough to supply 1.9 million U.S. homes with electricity. In all, as of April 2014 the Electric Reliability Council of Texas, which manages most of the Texas grid, was tracking interconnection requests by wind companies to add 27,000 megawatts of wind power.

In nine states, wind provides at least 12 percent of electricity. Iowa and South Dakota are each generating at least 26 percent of their electricity from wind. If Iowa succeeds in getting half of its electricity from wind farms, which the state wind industry says is possible by 2018 in the right policy environment, it will be the first state in the country to shift from coal to wind as its primary source of electricity.

Warren Buffett's MidAmerican Energy Company brought Iowa closer to that milestone when it announced in December 2013 that it had ordered $1.9 billion worth of wind turbines from Siemens for use in the state. Half were in operation by the end of 2014. The remainder will be online by the end of 2015. In total, the wind farms will add 1,000 megawatts of wind capacity.

More and more, Native American tribes are looking to develop the wind resources on their reservations. At the June 2013 Clinton Global Initiative America meeting, six Sioux tribes announced plans to build one of the largest U.S. wind complexes. Two more tribes have since joined the effort, so the 1,000- to 2,000-megawatt Oceti Sakowin Power Project will now span eight reservations in South Dakota. Revenue from selling the electricity under long-term agreements with outside purchasers will be used for economic development in tribal communities. Project manager Caroline Herron notes that a number of the tribes are also looking to develop their solar and geothermal resources.

Meanwhile, in Oklahoma five tribes are collaborating to build a 153-megawatt wind farm. It will be half-owned by the Cherokee Nation, with the remainder on land belonging to the Kaw Nation, Otoe-Missouria Tribe, Pawnee Nation, and Ponca Nation. Cherokee chief Bill

John Baker said, "The Cherokee Nation expects to play a key role in Oklahoma's emerging wind energy industry."

Also turning to the wind is India, soon to be the world's most populous country. Its 20,000 megawatts of wind generating capacity put it fifth on the world list. New Delhi plans to invest roughly $8 billion in grid transmission upgrades to accommodate much more wind and solar power. Part of this effort is aimed at the 300 million people in India who do not yet have electricity. The National Wind Energy Mission under the Modi government is expected to set an official goal of 60,000 megawatts of wind generating capacity by 2022.

In Latin America, Brazil, with 200 million people, is by far the regional leader in wind resource development. At the start of 2014, it had 3,500 megawatts of wind generating capacity, enough to supply 8 million homes. The goal is to boost capacity nearly fivefold to 17,000 megawatts by 2022. Given its wealth of wind—and the fact that wind developers often win contracts to build new power capacity by bidding below coal or natural gas projects there—Brazil could surpass this goal.

Chile, with a long mountain ridge paralleling its long coastline, is also beginning to harness its abundant wind resources. Its 115-megawatt El Arrayán wind farm, some 250 miles north of Santiago, began generating electricity in June 2014. High electricity prices and a heavy reliance on fuel imports for electricity generation make building up renewable power capacity quite attractive in Chile. As Bloomberg New Energy Finance analyst Ethan Zindler pointed out in a recent interview, "Clean energy is the low-cost option in a lot of [emerging markets]. The technologies are cost-competitive right now. Not in the future, but right now."

After a late start, wind generation is now expanding rapidly in parts of Eastern Europe. Poland, notorious for its heavy dependence on coal, not only now has 3,400 megawatts of wind power, but the wind segment of the energy economy is growing fast. Romania is close behind with 2,600 megawatts of wind generating capacity. Bridging Europe and Asia, Turkey has great wind power ambitions, with its long, wind-rich coastline and wind-swept Anatolian plateau. Although it had only 3,000 megawatts of wind generating capacity at the start of 2014, Turkey plans to have 20,000 megawatts within a decade, enough to meet one fourth of its current electricity needs.

Although the harnessing of the earth's wind resources has been limited mostly to resources over land, a growing number of countries are now also tapping winds offshore, where they are often stronger. Denmark built the world's first offshore facility, a 5-megawatt wind farm in the Baltic Sea. At the start of 2014, the country's offshore capacity was close to 1,300 megawatts.

For years, Denmark was the world leader in this field, but in 2007 it ceded this position to the United Kingdom. By January 2014, the United Kingdom had nearly 3,700 megawatts of offshore wind—half the world's total and enough to power more than 2 million homes. The London Array offshore wind farm, with 630 megawatts of generating capacity, is the world's largest offshore wind installation. Other European countries that are beginning to seriously develop their offshore wind resources include Belgium, currently with 570 megawatts, and Germany, with 520 megawatts. The Germans expect to install an additional 2,500 megawatts of offshore capacity by the end of 2015, with a target of 6,500 megawatts by 2020.

In May 2014, a consortium consisting of European companies and Northland Power Inc., a Canadian power producer, announced it was moving ahead with a 600-megawatt wind farm 50 miles off the coast of the Netherlands. This project is part of an effort by the Dutch to get 14 percent of their energy from renewable sources by 2020.

Close behind the leading European countries is China, with 430 megawatts of offshore wind power installed by early 2014. Although China has come late to offshore wind, as of mid-2014 it had 1,000 megawatts under construction, with another 44 projects totaling 10,000 megawatts in the pipeline. Japan, South Korea, and Viet Nam are among the other countries developing offshore wind resources.

Countries with shallow coastal waters have a distinct advantage in developing large-scale offshore wind resources. These include, for example, countries around the North Sea, the Baltic Sea, and the Gulf of Mexico, as well as the U.S. East Coast.

The U.S. Department of Energy estimates that the shallow waters off the East Coast are capable of hosting 530,000 megawatts of wind generating capacity, enough to satisfy 40 percent of the country's electricity needs. If the wind potential of deeper East Coast waters, as well as the Great Lakes, the Gulf of Mexico, and the Pacific Coast, are included, then offshore wind could easily meet all U.S. electricity needs. About a dozen U.S. offshore wind project proposals are moving ahead, although by late 2014 only two of them had begun early-stage construction: the 470-megawatt Cape Wind project off Massachusetts and Rhode Island's 30-megawatt Block Island wind farm.

In June 2014, U.S. Interior Secretary Sally Jewell and Massachusetts Governor Deval Patrick announced that more than 740,000 acres off the coast of Massachusetts would be designated for offshore wind development and auctioned off as four lease areas. Governor Patrick sees offshore wind as an economic growth opportunity for his state, noting that it has no coal or oil reserves: "We sit at the end of the energy pipeline and we are held in some sense hostage to the fossil fuel rollercoaster.... Offshore wind...represents an opportunity to create our own Massachusetts-made energy."

This announcement added to the five commercial wind energy leases already granted for areas off the costs of Delaware, Massachusetts, Rhode Island, and Virginia. Then in August 2014 the Department of the Interior awarded two more leases, both offshore of Maryland, totaling nearly 80,000 acres.

Getting the electricity generated by offshore wind farms to population centers presents the challenge of installing the substations, laying the cables, and connecting the turbines at sea. The world's largest offshore wind farms to date have been connected to onshore grids via subsea high-voltage alternating current (HVAC) cables. These include the United Kingdom's 630-megawatt London Array and 500-megawatt Greater Gabbard wind farms, as well as Denmark's 400-megawatt Anholt project. None of these is more than 20 miles off the coast.

Offshore developers in the North and Baltic Seas are now looking farther out for even stronger and steadier wind resources. As the distance from shore grows, so do electricity transmission losses from HVAC cables, which means that at a certain point the much more efficient high-voltage direct current (HVDC) lines are needed. Navigant Research projects that by 2020, HVDC cables will deliver the output from up to 30,000 megawatts of offshore wind farms.

TenneT, the company in charge of transmission systems in the German part of the North Sea, has contracted with firms to develop nine offshore stations that receive the electricity generated by wind farm clusters and then send it via HVDC lines to the German grid. As of mid-2014, Siemens had built four of these hubs and had been awarded a fifth; all told, these will be able to accommodate wind farms with a combined 3,800 megawatts of capacity. The Switzerland-based power and automation firm ABB was contracted to build three of the other four hubs, good for an additional 2,100 megawatts. The 400-megawatt BARD wind farm, which began generating in 2012, sends electricity roughly 80 miles to shore through one of these ABB stations.

As Germany pursues its *Energiewende*—an "energy transition" from nuclear and fossil fuels to renewables for 80 percent of electricity and 60 percent of total energy by 2050—the offshore wind grid will feed into a cleaner, more efficient grid that is taking shape on land. Along with Germany's three other transmission system operators, TenneT is planning three HVDC transmission corridors running hundreds of miles from windier northern Germany to the country's industrial and more nuclear-reliant south. The western-most corridor, for example, would run 400 miles from the North Sea port town of Emden down to 40 miles northwest of Stuttgart, near the Philippsburg nuclear reactor that is due to close in 2019.

This German grid based on renewable power sources—primarily wind and solar—could eventually be part of a European Supergrid. Envisioned by a coalition of companies—including some of the biggest names in energy, such as Siemens, ABB, General Electric, and Alstom—the Supergrid would be a single-market European high-voltage electricity network delivering power from facilities like Spanish solar farms, Norwegian hydropower dams, and North Sea wind farms to wherever it is needed. It will take much more coordination and commitment among European countries to make this a reality.

Development of long-distance transmission also goes hand-in-hand with wind in the United States, where the strongest onshore wind resources tend to be found in more-remote areas. For example, in the wind-rich but sparsely populated state of Wyoming, a wind farm now planned by oil billionaire Philip Anschutz will soon be the largest U.S. facility under construction, with 3,000 megawatts of generating capacity. Called the Chokecherry and Sierra Madre Wind Energy Project, this wind farm will tie into one or more of several major transmission lines planned in Wyoming and will supply electricity to high-demand markets in California, Arizona, and Nevada. One candidate for this connection is the planned 725-mile, 3,000-megawatt TransWest Express transmission line—another Anschutz venture.

In Texas, a series of transmission projects linking windy West Texas and the Panhandle with populous areas like Dallas–Fort Worth was completed in early 2014. Some 460 megawatts now under construction in the Panhandle's Mariah wind complex will tie into these new lines. Mariah could eventually reach 6,000 megawatts of capacity or more. Already generating 8 percent of the electricity in Texas, wind farms are now poised to contribute even more to the power supply with these transmission lines in place. Other operational U.S. long-distance transmission lines include the Pacific Intertie, using highly efficient HVDC cables to link wind and hydropower resources in Washington and Oregon with California.

Among the most ambitious players in the U.S. transmission business today is Houston-based Clean Line Energy Partners. The group has proposed building five lines—four of them HVDC—with a combined length of 3,000 miles and the capacity to deliver 15,000 megawatts. For example, the Grain Belt Express Clean Line would link windy western Kansas to Missouri, Illinois, and Indiana. Another will connect the plains of northwest Iowa to Illinois and points eastward.

Perhaps the most exciting grid project under development is the proposed Tres Amigas Superstation electricity hub to be built in Clovis in eastern New Mexico. It will link the three major power grids of the United States: the Western Interconnection, which includes the West Coast, Arizona, and much of New Mexico; the Eastern Interconnection, which extends from the Atlantic Coast to the Rocky Mountains; and the Texas Interconnection. This initial linkage of the three grids will allow electricity to move from one part of the United States to another as conditions warrant. It is a landmark in the evolution of the new energy economy. By matching surpluses with deficits over a broader area than previously possible, electricity losses and consumer rates can both be lowered. Intermittent resources like wind and solar can be more easily balanced over a wider geography.

Beyond expanding wind power's reach into new areas, a leading source of growth in the wind energy sector is repowering: the replacement of older wind turbines with larger, more-productive ones. In one replacement project in California, 34 new 2.3-megawatt wind turbines replaced 438 small turbines that dated from the 1980s. Although the total generating capacity stayed roughly the same, the highly efficient new turbines produce more than twice as much electricity. In more-mature markets like California, Germany, Denmark, and Spain, repowering and refurbishing old turbines is supplying more power than brand-new wind farms do.

The impressive growth in world wind electricity generation is likely to continue in the years ahead, with an expanding share of the growth coming in developing countries. As wind technologies continue to advance and costs continue to decline, wind will emerge as a leading source of electricity.

Data, endnotes, and additional resources can be found at Earth Policy Institute, www.earth-policy.org.

7

Tapping the Earth's Heat

The temperature at the center of the earth is more than 10,000 degrees Fahrenheit (5,700 degrees Celsius), roughly the same as on the surface of the sun. As this geothermal energy radiates out from the earth's core and mantle, it can be converted into electricity or used directly to heat facilities like buildings and greenhouses.

Geothermal resources around the world are richest in areas of high tectonic activity. The so-called Ring of Fire, which encircles the Pacific Ocean, is one such zone. It includes the Andean countries (such as Chile, Peru, and Colombia), Central America, and the West Coast of the United States and Canada. On the other side of the Pacific, it includes Japan, China, the Philippines, and Indonesia. Another concentration of geothermal resources is found in the Great Rift Valley of Africa, encompassing Ethiopia, Kenya, Rwanda, Tanzania, and Uganda. The Eastern Mediterranean region is also well endowed.

But the geothermal capital of the world is Iceland. Straddling the Mid-Atlantic Ridge where the North American and Eurasian tectonic plates are spreading apart at a rate of about four fifths of an inch (2 centimeters) per year, this island of volcanoes is one of the most geologically active places on earth. Geothermal energy figures prominently in nearly every aspect of life in Iceland, from electricity generation and home heating to vegetable growing, fish farming, and bathing.

Many parts of Iceland have underground temperatures of up to 480 degrees Fahrenheit (250 degrees Celsius) within a mile of the surface—excellent conditions for geothermal power generation. With 660 megawatts of geothermal power capacity installed by early 2014, Iceland generates 29 percent of its electricity from the earth, the highest share in the world. (Hydropower accounts for nearly all of the rest.) Hot water and steam are brought from underground reservoirs to the earth's surface through wells drilled into porous rock. The steam from the reservoir or from the hot water drives a turbine to generate electricity. Because of its abundance of cheap geothermal electricity, Iceland has become a powerhouse of aluminum manufacturing, a very energy-intensive industry. Nearly 70 percent of Iceland's electricity goes to aluminum smelting.

Iceland's natural hot springs have been used for centuries, likely since settlement began some 1,100 years ago. Over the last 100 years or so, roughly 150 geothermally heated recreational swimming centers have been built in virtually every community nationwide. Most are public facilities operating year-round, many of them outdoors. Iceland's most famous tourist destination, the Blue Lagoon—which each year receives far more visitors than Iceland's population of 330,000—boasts an extensive series of pools ranging from 95 to 117 degrees Fahrenheit. They actually contain the brine released from the Svartsengi geothermal plant, which produces electricity and supplies hot water for residential use.

Geothermally heated water is sent from cogeneration plants like Svartsengi or from "low-temperature" (less than 300 degrees Fahrenheit) geothermal fields through a network of pipes to heat buildings. In 1970, over 50 percent of space heating in Iceland came from burning oil, while geothermal accounted for 43 percent. The government reacted to oil price hikes in that decade by giving priority to district heating expansion, and today geothermal energy provides nearly 90 percent of all space heating directly. About 10 percent is from electricity (also partially geothermally produced), and oil is now less than 1 percent of the total. The 184,000 residents of the capital, Reykjavik, warm themselves with geothermal district heating.

Iceland uses its geothermal resources in a wide variety of other ways. For example, nearly 13 million square feet of sidewalks, parking spaces, and streets, mostly in Reykjavik, are heated from below by warm water (often water that was already used to heat a building) to prevent icing and to ease snow removal. Direct uses of geothermal energy by industry include cement curing and salt production. Geothermal energy is used to heat 48 acres of greenhouses that produce vegetables, fruits, flowers, and other plants. In some 15–20 fish farming operations, Arctic char, salmon, and Senegalese sole are raised in geothermally heated water.

While Iceland is clearly a model, China leads the world in the amount of geothermal energy harnessed for direct use. China's installed capacity is estimated at 6,100 thermal megawatts, about 30 percent of the world total. Roughly half of this capacity is used for district heating, which has grown by a factor of five in China over the last decade. The rapid growth is owed in part to Icelandic expertise: Orka Energy, based in Reykjavik, teamed up with China's Sinopec Star Petroleum Co. to form Sinopec Green Energy Geothermal Development Co., Ltd. In late 2013 the partnership announced that it had tapped enough geothermal energy to heat 161 million square feet of space. It expects this figure to double by 2015. Another 40 percent of China's direct-use capacity is for hot baths and spas, with the remainder divided among fish farming, greenhouses, agriculture, and industry. Coming in a distant second on the world stage is Turkey, with 2,800 thermal megawatts of direct-use geothermal capacity as of 2014. More than one third of this is used to heat the country's numerous baths and spas, another quarter goes to district heating, and 20 percent heats an impressive 740 acres of greenhouses.

After Iceland (third in the world ranking of direct-use geothermal capacity, with 2,200 thermal megawatts) comes Japan, with 2,100 thermal megawatts. A geothermally rich country long known for its thousands of hot baths, Japan was an early leader in this field. Nearly 90 percent of the country's direct-use capacity serves the 2,000 spas, 5,000 public bathhouses, and 15,000 hotels that use nature's hot water. India, number five on the list, has developed 990 thermal megawatts of direct geothermal capacity, virtually all for bathing and swimming.

Italy, France, and Germany have also tapped their geothermal resources to heat both water and space. Half of Italy's 800 thermal megawatts of direct-use capacity is for bathing and swimming. It has some district heating, for example in Tuscany, but this has not been widely developed. The opposite is true for both France and Germany, where district heating makes up at least 80 percent of the geothermal direct-use capacity. The Paris metropolitan area has an estimated 170,000 households that are geothermally heated, with 10,000 more expected by 2015.

To the east, Hungary stands out for its direct use of geothermal energy. Bathing and swimming uses account for up to 44 percent of its 615 thermal megawatts of direct-use capacity. Geothermal energy heats 1,200 swimming pools there during the winter. And 173 acres of greenhouses get heat from 193 geothermal wells.

Geothermal direct-use applications in the United States, also with 615 thermal megawatts of capacity, include greenhouses, industrial process heat, and district heating. The first U.S. city to turn to geothermal energy for district heating—in 1892—was Boise, Idaho, a city that now has some 214,000 people. It uses this subterranean heat source to warm hundreds of buildings, including the Idaho Statehouse. In 2014, Boise State University started using geothermal energy to heat nine of its buildings. Other U.S. cities with geothermal district heating include Reno, Nevada, and Klamath Falls, Oregon.

At Ball State University in Indiana, the school's two remaining coal-fired boilers were closed on March 19, 2014, to be replaced by geothermal energy. Jim Lowe, director of engineering, construction, and operations, calculates that using geothermal heating and cooling to replace the 33,000 tons of coal burned each year will save the university $2 million annually while cutting its carbon footprint in half.

The United States is also among the 21 countries that use geothermal energy for fish farming. In California, for example, Pacific Aquafarms produces tilapia, catfish, silver carp, and striped bass year-round in geothermally heated ponds and tanks. The firm supplies some 2 million pounds of fish each year to live-fish markets in the greater Los Angeles and San Diego areas and to lakes stocked for recreational fishing.

In Israel's Negev Desert, 100-degree Fahrenheit brackish water from underground is used to raise tilapia, catfish, sea bass, red drum, and barramundi. Rich in nutrients from fish waste, the water from the fish farms is then used to irrigate olive groves, date palms, and alfalfa in this water-scarce country.

Beyond district heating, aquaculture, hot baths, and the other direct-use applications just described, there are ground-source heat pumps, also known as geothermal heat pumps. These systems take advantage of the remarkable stability of the earth's temperature just a few feet from the surface, using it as a source of heat in the winter when the air temperature is low and as a source of cooling in the summer when the air temperature is high. The great attraction of this technology is that it uses 25–50 percent less electricity than would be needed with conventional heating and cooling systems. Unlike the other direct uses of geothermal energy, heat pumps can serve homes, schools, and other structures virtually anywhere in the world, even places without deep high-temperature resources. The estimated worldwide capacity of ground-source heat pumps is some 50,000 thermal megawatts.

While 82 countries report using geothermal energy directly, a comparatively modest 24 countries convert energy from the earth into electricity. Over one fourth of the world's installed geothermal electricity generating capacity—which stood at 11,700 megawatts by the start of 2014—is in the United States. Another one fourth is in the Philippines and Indonesia. Italy and New Zealand round out the top five countries. Next up in the capacity ranking are Mexico, Iceland, Japan, Kenya, and Turkey.

In terms of the importance of geothermal power as a share of national electricity generation, however, the world ranking changes dramatically. Iceland, as noted earlier, tops the list. Not far behind, with 26 percent of its electricity coming from the earth, is El Salvador. In Kenya, the share is about 19 percent. The Philippines, Costa Rica, and New Zealand all get close to 15 percent of their electricity from geothermal sources. Also ranking high on the list are Papua New Guinea, Nicaragua, and Indonesia.

Several of these countries could go much further in harnessing their resources. The U.S.-based Geothermal Energy Association (GEA) has identified some 40 countries that could satisfy all their electricity needs with geothermal power alone. Among these are Costa Rica, Ecuador, El Salvador, Ethiopia, Indonesia, Kenya, Peru, the Philippines, Tanzania, and Uganda. Together these countries are home to 860 million people, or 12 percent of the world's population.

The United States has 3,440 megawatts of installed geothermal electric generating capacity, enough to power some 1.4 million homes. For several decades, U.S. geothermal power was confined largely to the Geysers project north of San Francisco. With nearly 1,500 megawatts of generating capacity, this is easily the world's largest geothermal generating complex. But now the United States is experiencing a geothermal renaissance. Some 124 power plants under development in 12 states are expected to add roughly 1,000 megawatts to U.S. geothermal capacity. As of April 2014, states developing projects of at least 20 megawatts each include Alaska, California, Colorado, Idaho, Nevada, Oregon, and Utah.

Most of the new facilities being developed in the United States today are "binary" plants. Hot water from the earth heats a second fluid like isobutane, which has a lower boiling point. When the fluid vaporizes, the vapor drives a turbine to generate electricity. Whereas temperatures above 350 degrees Fahrenheit were historically needed to generate electricity at geothermal power plants, binary plants can use geothermal resources at around 210 degrees Fahrenheit. The potential to use such lower-temperature geothermal fields for power generation is also helping countries like Germany begin to bring geothermal energy into the power mix.

Currently, California and Nevada have over 95 percent of the total U.S. geothermal generating capacity. Utah, Hawaii, Oregon, and Idaho account for nearly all the remainder. In California, CalEnergy—a subsidiary of Warren Buffett's MidAmerican Renewables—announced in May 2014 a plan to invest $1 billion to sustain its 10 geothermal facilities around the Salton Sea. The GEA estimates that roughly 50 percent of California's available geothermal resource remains untapped. The comparable figure for Nevada is 60 percent.

Nationwide, the U.S. Geological Survey estimates that 42,000 megawatts of geothermal electricity generating capacity could be developed, enough to supply 30 million American homes. In other words, 90 percent of U.S. geothermal power potential is waiting to be tapped.

The Philippines, currently the world's number two generator of electricity from geothermal sources, is also planning new projects. A 40-megawatt project in Oriental Mindoro Province that was set to begin drilling in late 2014 is expected to lower local electricity bills by some 40 percent. The Philippines' Department of Energy aims to increase total geothermal power capacity from 1,900 megawatts to 3,300 megawatts by 2030.

Indonesia, a country with 127 active volcanoes and thus a wealth of underground energy to harness, has so far developed just 1,340 megawatts of geothermal generating capacity. Although geothermal power has grown slowly there in recent years, it is picking up momentum. A 330-megawatt project in North Sumatra began construction in June 2014. Key regulatory reforms that year opened up new areas to geothermal exploration and made projects more financially attractive. In late 2014, Jakarta announced that 25 project sites would be open for bidding in 2015. The near-term goal is to nearly quadruple geothermal power capacity to 4,900 megawatts by 2019. By 2025, Indonesia intends to have 10,000 megawatts of geothermal capacity, enough to cover one third of its current electricity consumption.

The huge geothermal potential in Indonesia is fortuitous, since its oil production has declined by half over the last two decades, transforming it from an oil exporter into an oil importer in recent years. Pertamina, the state oil company, has been the principal geothermal power developer. As Pertamina shifts its development efforts from oil to geothermal, it could become the first oil company—state-owned or independent—to make the transition from oil to renewable energy.

Japan could develop more than 80,000 megawatts of geothermally generated electricity—enough to meet over half of its electricity needs. Unfortunately, today it has only 500 megawatts of geothermal generating capacity, due in part to a long-time ban on geothermal development in national parks and monuments, areas housing much of the country's geothermal resources. In March 2012, one year after the Fukushima nuclear accident, the government changed that law, giving the green light to small-scale geothermal projects at several park sites, with close governmental oversight. A feed-in tariff for geothermal was also introduced in 2012, guaranteeing the producer a long-term purchase price for all electricity sent to the grid. As a result, Japan now has 47 projects under development.

New Zealand, a country with 4.5 million people and the world's largest boiling lake, generates about 14 percent of its electricity from geothermal power plants. This share is set to rise because of the 166-megawatt Te Mihi plant inaugurated on the country's North Island in August 2014 by Contact Energy, a large power provider. Because of the climbing cost of natural gas in New Zealand, the company has been replacing some of its gas-fired generation with geothermal power. Te Mihi will allow the company to produce even less gas-fired electricity. Contact's chief executive Dennis Barnes said in late 2014, "I used to have a gas bill that was $300 million to $400 million—next year I'll have a gas bill that is $100 million. I've replaced that [gas] with...geothermal." Contact is not the only power company in New Zealand ditching natural gas. Mighty River Power, another large electricity provider, has replaced some of its gas-fired capacity with geothermal plants and wind farms in recent years as well. In fact, it appears that geothermal power is replacing natural gas as New Zealand's number two electricity source behind hydropower: for the 12 months up through October 30, 2014, geothermal accounted for 16.3 percent of the generation mix, edging out natural gas at 15.8 percent.

Back in the northern hemisphere, Italy—the world's number four producer of geothermal electricity—had 880 megawatts installed by the start of 2014. Larderello, the site where geothermal energy was first harnessed to generate electricity in 1904, still hosts a power plant that began operation in 1913.

Turkey, with just 220 megawatts of geothermal power installed by the beginning of 2014, is adding handsomely to its capacity. In December 2014, Alexander Richter, founder of the geothermal news website ThinkGeoEnergy.com, reported that Turkey had reached 400 megawatts of installed capacity, and that dozens of geothermal developers had enough projects in the pipeline to nearly double that total again.

In the Great Rift countries in Africa, Kenya has emerged as the early leader. It now has over 250 megawatts of geothermal electricity generating capacity and will soon add several hundred more megawatts. For the longer term, Kenya has set the ambitious goal of 5,000 megawatts by 2030. In a country where only 19 percent of the population has access to electricity, this would be a welcome development. Neighboring Ethiopia is also setting its geothermal sights high. In 2014, the Icelandic company Reykjavik Geothermal began drilling the first of two 500-megawatt phases of the Corbetti geothermal project. To put this planned 1,000-megawatt capacity in perspective, Ethiopia's current generating capacity from all sources is about 2,000 megawatts, mostly in the form of hydropower.

In Central America, Costa Rica is aiming to be carbon-neutral by 2021, with 100 percent of its electricity generated from renewable sources. With more than 90 percent of its electricity already renewably produced—about 70 percent hydropower, 14 percent geothermal, 5 percent wind, and slightly less than 2 percent biomass—Costa Rica is well on its way. But its heavy dependence on hydro leads to electricity rationing and the use offor oil-fired power late in the dry season. The government is looking to add to its 200 megawatts of installed geothermal capacity to help address this seasonal problem. Three 55-megawatt geothermal plants planned for the northwestern province of Guanacaste, financed largely by the Japan International Cooperation Agency, will generate enough electricity for 200,000 Costa Rican homes.

Exploratory drilling for geothermal resources in El Salvador began in 1968. Despite political turmoil in the subsequent decades, including a bloody civil war in the 1980s, two major geothermal fields were developed that today generate 26 percent of the country's electricity. El Salvador's goal is to boost this share to 40 percent. In late 2014, however, Italy's Enel Green Power sold to the government its shares of La Geo, the company that owns and operates El Salvador's geothermal plants, making it fully state-owned. It is unclear how this will affect the country's geothermal expansion.

Globally, with some 60 geothermal power plants under construction in 2014, GEA expects at least 1,400 megawatts of new geothermal generating capacity to come online over the next few years. Among the countries housing these new projects are Kenya, Mexico, New Zealand, Nicaragua, Turkey, and the United States. Other countries where geothermal power development could move forward include Argentina, Australia, Azerbaijan, Chile, Germany, Guatemala, Malaysia, Rwanda, Thailand, Uganda, and Zambia.

As with both wind and solar, the principal expense in harnessing geothermal energy is the up-front cost. For developing geothermal power, this means well drilling. Exploratory wells often reach a mile or so deep. The test-drilling phase is both expensive and uncertain—it may account for 15 percent of the project's capital cost, with no guarantee that a viable site will be found—typically making financing difficult. Once a field is discovered, the major cost is for drilling to reach the hot water and steam below the earth's surface. After a plant is built, operation and maintenance costs are relatively low—importantly, because there is no fuel cost. Over the life of the generator, geothermal plants are often cost-competitive with all other power sources.

Developers are still finding new conventional reservoirs with sufficient hot water or steam for geothermal power plants, but a relatively new technology—enhanced geothermal systems (EGS)—holds the greatest potential for expanding electricity generation from the earth's heat worldwide. Where hot rock resources exist but the rock is too dry or impermeable for conventional geothermal technology to work, EGS injects water deep underground to reopen existing fissures and create a new geothermal reservoir. A second well brings heated water to the surface, where it flashes into steam and drives a geothermal turbine.

EGS technology is adapted from the oil and gas industry's hydraulic fracturing techniques, but there are key differences. Writing in *Science* magazine in 2013, Joseph Moore and Stuart Simmons of the Energy & Geoscience Institute at the University of Utah noted that "the target geologic formations are deeper, no toxic chemicals are used, and the risk of adverse environmental impacts is much lower" than with fracking for oil and gas.

At this early stage, the few EGS projects that have come online are quite small. The first grid-connected EGS facility, a 2-megawatt plant in France, began operating in 2008. In Australia, a 1-megawatt pilot project reaching roughly 2.5 miles below the earth's surface started up in 2013. And that same year in the United States, the geothermal firm Ormat Technologies Inc. brought online its 1.7-megawatt Desert Peak system in Nevada. Built alongside an existing 18-megawatt geothermal plant, early results show that this EGS facility can boost the electricity production from underperforming wells by close to 40 percent.

Desert Peak's initial success is promising, but it only hints at the magnitude of potential electricity generation from EGS. A team assembled by the Massachusetts Institute of Technology wrote in 2006 that EGS could provide 100,000 megawatts of generating capacity in the United States alone by 2050. The U.S. Geological Survey estimates the country's total EGS potential at more than 500,000 megawatts. For comparison, the world as a whole is estimated to have a conventional geothermal potential of about 200,000 megawatts.

In 2014, the U.S. Department of Energy (DOE) launched an ambitious initiative called FORGE—Frontier Observatory for Research in Geothermal Energy—with the stated goal of reaching the 100,000-megawatt mark. Under DOE direction, FORGE will bring together industry, academia, and the national laboratories to develop an EGS research and demonstration site. The aim is to test EGS methods and technologies, to model reservoirs, and to collect and share data in order to greatly reduce the risk and cost of EGS, allowing the technology to take off. This will be an international effort to some extent, with participation from Japan, Switzerland, Taiwan, and others.

One of the strong selling points of geothermal power is that it is a steady, reliable source of electricity, able to run virtually non-stop. But perhaps an even better selling point, as the energy transition proceeds and as more wind and solar installations connect to the grid, is that geothermal plants can ramp up generation quickly as needed. This reduces the need for expensive fossil fuel generators to be on standby for when the wind stops blowing or night falls. In places endowed with enough underground heat to develop geothermal power plants, the potential benefits are huge.

Data, endnotes, and additional resources can be found at Earth Policy Institute, www.earth-policy.org.

8

Hydropower: Past and Future

In 1966, at the age of 72, Mao Zedong famously swam in Asia's longest river, the Yangtze, to demonstrate his vigor and the strength of the Cultural Revolution. A dip in the fast-moving waters a decade earlier had inspired him to write a poem about how a dam on the Yangtze—a project that had been envisioned for flood control as early as 1919 by the founder of the Republic of China, Sun Yat-sen—could change the world. In 1994, some 18 years after Mao's death, construction began on what would become the largest hydroelectric project ever seen: the Three Gorges Dam.

First online in 2003 and fully completed in 2012, the 600-foot-tall Three Gorges Dam has an estimated electricity generating capacity of 22,500 megawatts. Its annual output of some 83 million megawatt-hours is equal to the power from burning 45 million tons of coal or running 12 nuclear reactors. Yet despite its major electricity contribution, the monumental dam—like many of the 300 mega-dams worldwide—has had a profound environmental, social, and economic impact.

The problems associated with the Three Gorges Dam

are highly visible. Its construction flooded 244 square miles and displaced over 1.4 million people. The Chinese government's promise to provide them with a home and life after relocation comparable to their previous livelihoods in economic terms has simply not materialized. The new reservoir has decimated plant and animal species unique to China and continues to trigger seismic activity and deadly landslides. The total bill has yet to be paid, but it could reach some $88 billion, not including the full environmental and human damage.

China's State Council, the equivalent of the U.S. Cabinet, has publicly recognized some of the project's shortcomings, stating that "although the Three Gorges project provides huge comprehensive benefits, urgent problems must be resolved regarding the smooth relocation of residents, ecological protection, and geological disaster prevention."

Around the world, more than 150 countries are grappling with hydropower's costs and benefits as they tap the energy in falling water to help run their economies. Of the world's 45,000 large dams—those standing more than four stories high—some 8,600 are equipped to generate electricity. In 1980 hydropower accounted for 20 percent of global electricity production. Since then the share has fallen to 16 percent, about enough to power the United States.

Global hydroelectric generating capacity in 2013 totaled 1 million megawatts. New dams are adding roughly 30,000 megawatts a year. Since 1965, the world's hydroelectric generation has expanded fourfold, growing steadily at about 2.8 percent a year through 2003 and then increasing to 3.7 percent between 2003 and 2013. The recent acceleration was boosted by a string of new large projects coming online in China.

Indeed, although hydroelectricity use is widespread, most of the generation is concentrated in a handful of large countries. With half the world's large dams, China is out in front, having nearly quadrupled its hydropower output between 2000 and 2012. China generates nearly as much electricity from hydropower as the next three countries—Brazil, Canada, and the United States—combined. After these three come Russia and India, followed by Norway, Venezuela, Japan, and France.

Many smaller countries get all or nearly all of their electricity from rivers. Paraguay, for example, gets 100 percent of its electricity from hydro generation. For Ethiopia, the figure is 99 percent. With work now under way on the 6,000-megawatt Grand Ethiopian Renaissance Dam on the Blue Nile, one of Africa's costliest infrastructure projects, this country's heavy dependence on hydropower will remain high even as energy demand climbs. Other countries that get nearly all their electricity from hydropower include Bhutan, the Democratic Republic of the Congo, Lesotho, Mozambique, Nepal, Norway, and Zambia.

Venezuela depends on hydropower for 60–70 percent of its electricity, which comes as somewhat of a surprise since it is a leading oil producer. Its Guri Dam, which was constructed in two phases between 1963 and 1986, has a generating capacity of more than 10,000 megawatts. It is to Venezuela's advantage to use hydro-generated electricity as much as possible so that it can export its oil. Hydropower also supplies over half the electricity in Austria, Ecuador, New Zealand, Peru, and Switzerland— all countries with mountainous topography.

Brazil has a high hydropower ranking thanks to its abundance of rivers, including the vast network of rivers in the Amazon basin that take water from the Andes to the Atlantic Ocean. Hydroelectric dams typically supply roughly 80 percent of the country's electricity. Among them is the Itaipu Dam located in the southern part of the country, which is easily the world's most productive dam. Its 20 generating units each have a capacity of 700 megawatts. Despite having a smaller capacity, Itaipu generally outperforms China's Three Gorges because of a more consistent year-round flow. Its record-breaking 2013 production of 98.6 million megawatt-hours of electricity could power the global economy for almost two days. Itaipu alone supplies 17 percent of Brazil's electricity and 75 percent of Paraguay's.

Like Brazil, Canada has many rivers—from its easternmost province of Newfoundland to British Columbia on its Pacific coast. Hydropower accounts for close to 60 percent of Canada's electricity consumption, and several of its dams rank among the world's largest. The Robert-Bourassa Dam on the La Grande River in northern Quebec stands as tall as a 53-story building and has a generating capacity of 5,616 megawatts. The 2,790 megawatt-W.A.C. Bennett Dam on the Peace River in British Columbia created the Williston Lake when it was built in the 1960s. It is one of 31 hydroelectric generating stations that produce 95 percent of that province's electricity.

Since Canada covers such a vast geographic area but has only 35 million people, it is well positioned to export surplus electricity to the United States, much of it going south from Ontario to New England and densely populated New York State. Canadian exports meet the electricity needs of roughly 10 million Americans.

Canada is not the only country to export a surplus of hydroelectricity. For Bhutan, a small and sparsely populated country of just 766,000 people in the eastern Himalayas, hydropower accounts for one fifth of the gross domestic product. Since the country produces far more hydroelectricity than it can consume, it sells the surplus to neighboring power-hungry India. Bhutan is building still more dams to expand electricity exports. For the

Bhutanese economy, electricity is the principal export and a major source of foreign exchange earnings.

Two of the world's largest dams in terms of reservoir size are located in Russia, where hydropower accounts for 17 percent of the country's electricity portfolio. Russia's largest source of hydropower is the 6,000-megawatt Krasnoyarsk Dam on the Yenisey River, which, like most of Russia's rivers, flows north into the Arctic Ocean. The Bratsk Dam, in Siberia, stands more than 410 feet high. Constructed between 1954 and 1964, it has a generating capacity of 4,500 megawatts.

The world's most voluminous reservoir is Lake Kariba, created by a dam on the Zambezi River in Zimbabwe. The dam supports a generating capacity of 1,470 megawatts, accounting for roughly 60 percent of hydropower generation—the principal source of electricity—in Zimbabwe and Zambia.

Another of the world's largest reservoirs is Lake Volta, created by the Akosombo Dam located on the Volta River in Ghana. This vast lake, behind a dam some 374 feet tall, contains a wealth of fish that provide livelihoods for some 300,000 local fishers. Despite the reservoir's huge size, the dam has a generating capacity of only 1,020 megawatts.

Every country has its own hydrological story. For the United States, the 10 largest dams were all built between 1930 and 1975. The Hoover Dam, built on the Colorado River in Nevada and completed in 1936, was a product of the public works projects of the Great Depression. So too was the Grand Coulee Dam—the nation's largest—completed in 1941 on the Columbia River in the state of Washington. With a generating capacity of 6,800 megawatts, it can satisfy the power needs of some 2.3 million homes. Construction of these two dams was an important part of U.S. economic history, creating jobs during the height of the Depression.

Hydropower accounts for 7 percent of U.S. electricity generation and 51 percent of what is considered to be renewable. The top hydroelectric generating states are Washington, Oregon, California, and New York, followed by Alabama, Tennessee, Montana, and Idaho. Regionally, the Northwest has the largest share of U.S. hydropower capacity. Much of it comes from dams on the Columbia River, which originates in the Canadian Rockies and flows through Washington and Oregon en route to the Pacific Ocean. The generating capacity of dams on the Columbia and its tributaries, including the huge Grand Coulee Dam, totals 29,000 megawatts and accounted for 44 percent of U.S. hydroelectric generation in 2012.

Altogether the United States has more than 80,000 dams of varying sizes that have been built on rivers and small streams. Fewer than 3 percent of these, however, are used to generate electricity; the bulk were constructed for flood control, irrigation, or turning wheels on mills that are no longer operating. Installing turbines and converting this water flow into electricity can provide some of the cheapest power available from any source. Senator Ed Markey from Massachusetts, a member of the Senate Environment and Public Works Committee, has noted that "with thousands of existing dams currently not creating any power, existing dams in need of upgrades, and new technologies being developed to safely capture river currents, an additional 60,000 megawatts [of hydro generation] is achievable within the next 15 years." For reference, this is equal to the generating capacity of 60 nuclear power reactors.

The Oak Ridge National Laboratory estimates much more conservatively that 54,000 existing U.S. dams that are not yet equipped to generate electricity could be renovated to produce an additional 12,100 megawatts of electricity. Much of this potential is concentrated in the Southeast and lower Midwest, where neither solar nor wind energy resources are well developed yet. At the same time that the U.S. government is exploring options for repowering or upgrading existing dams, decommissioning of older dams is freeing up some impeded rivers. The conservation group American Rivers calculates that over the last quarter-century nearly 900 dams have been taken down in the United States. Since 2007, U.S. waterways have lost an average of at least one dam each week, primarily in New England and the Great Lakes vicinity, as well as in California and the Pacific Northwest. The dismantled dams are mostly smaller, not producing much if any power, and oftentimes are costlier to maintain than to remove.

As dams have come down, fish and other wildlife have returned. The largest American dam removals thus far have been two on Washington State's Elwha River: the 108-foot high Elwha Dam, which came down in 2011, and the 210-foot tall Glines Canyon Dam, in 2014. After disrupting the river flow for over a century, the dams' demise is bringing hope for a renewed salmon run. Europe is also restoring a number of rivers, including tearing down dams on France's longest river, the Loire, and Spain's large Douro River.

These dam removals serve as a reminder of the pros and cons of hydropower as an energy source. Its principal attractions are that it is renewable and usually reliable. It meshes nicely with wind and solar energy, since it can run nearly continuously, as weather allows, or be ramped up quickly to offset fluctuations in wind and solar production. Beyond power generation, dams can also provide water storage, flood control, and irrigation water. Thus in some cases, in addition to providing energy security, they can also contribute to food security.

Hydropower's drawbacks, however, are causing some people to reexamine its role. Hydropower dams and the reservoirs they create generally flood vast areas, displacing whole communities of people and inundating historical sites and cultural legacies. The flooding can eliminate local plant and animal species, reducing the biological diversity of the planet. Dams also weaken the resilience of river ecosystems, impede sediment flows, and threaten the stability of downstream land. They can cause downstream lakes and wetlands to shrink or disappear and can interrupt the movement of fish and other creatures. Water in reservoirs and rivers slowed by dams warms more quickly than water in free-flowing rivers, threatening temperature-sensitive aquatic life. So while irrigation from a reservoir's water can increase crop production, the dam may cause the collapse of fisheries, important sources of protein.

Hydropower production itself is subject to disruption by drought. This was recently seen in Brazil, which in 2014 endured electricity blackouts when hit by the worst drought in 80 years. In the same year, severe drought in California halved hydropower's contribution to the state's electricity output. Precipitation extremes—both droughts and floods—increase the risks that hydropower may not pay dividends. Nigeria's Kainji Dam has missed its hydropower production target by as much as 70 percent due to water fluctuations from droughts and floods.

Although it is renewable, hydropower production is not climate-neutral. The vast amount of concrete used to build a megadam has a large carbon footprint. Less obvious are the emissions of methane—a potent global warming gas—from decomposing plant material in flooded reservoirs and trapped behind dams. The full impact varies depending on geography and local conditions, but some studies have shown that the climate impact of hydropower reservoirs can exceed that from power plants that burn fossil fuels. Furthermore, building dams and their reservoirs can trigger seismic activity. Over 100 earthquakes worldwide have been linked to reservoir-induced seismicity, including the devastating May 2008 quake in China's Sichuan Province that killed a reported 80,000 people. Christian Klose, a researcher at the consultancy Think Geohazards, says that the massive amount of water that accumulated behind the Zipingpu Dam, located a mile from a major fault zone, "amplified the strain on the earth's crust." A number of studies by U.S. and Chinese scientists, drawing on experience in China and elsewhere, agree that the dam—a government project—could have caused the 7.9-magnitude earthquake. A 2013 magnitude 7.0 quake on the same fault line may also have been dam-induced.

Dam-building strains economies as well as geology. A 2013 study by an Oxford University team warns developing countries that turning to hydropower to meet electricity needs is a gamble. Brazil's enormous $20-billion Itaipu Dam, for instance, experienced a 240 percent cost overrun by the time it came online in 1984, a sum so large that it left the country financially impaired for three decades. The Oxford survey of 245 dams built around the world since 1934 showed that the final cost of building dams typically comes in at about double the original budget. In addition, 80 percent of projects failed to meet their construction schedule.

Two of the authors underline these risks in a *Wall Street Journal* op-ed, noting that "because megadams take 8.6 years on average and often more than 10 years to build [not including the full development time], these projects don't ease urgent energy crises. The long lead time makes the projects especially vulnerable to currency volatility, inflation, political tensions, swings in water availability and electricity prices." The bottom line is that in building dams, as with nuclear power plants, cost overruns and schedule failure are the rule, not the exception. Governments may be better off choosing more flexible infrastructure—like wind and solar power—to aid their development.

Despite the economic downsides, new hydropower development may be on an upturn. Looking at proposed projects around the world, a team led by Christiane Zarfl, now of the Universität Tübingen, and Alexander Lumsdon of the Freie Universität Berlin counted at least 3,700 dams of over 1 megawatt capacity planned or under construction around the world, mostly in emerging economies. Were they all to be built, global hydroelectric capacity would increase from close to 1 million megawatts to 1.7 million megawatts. While most of the dams would be small or mid-sized, the 847 proposed large dams (those over 100 megawatts) account for 93 percent of this potential power capacity increase.

This corresponds to the International Energy Agency's projections for hydroelectric generation increasing 70 percent by 2040. A fifth of this growth is expected in China, which has some 200 potential hydropower projects in the pipeline, mostly in its southwest. The rest of the projected hydropower growth would come from a scattering of large dams being built in countries such as Brazil, Pakistan, and Turkey and in sub-Saharan Africa, as well as from numerous small hydro facilities under construction in southern Asia and Latin America.

Brazil is working on a number of dams in the Amazon. One of the three large ones under development, the Belo Monte, is expected to have a robust power capacity of 14,000 megawatts. Like many of the planned Amazonian dams, it has proved contentious because it would displace native communities and disrupt an incredibly biodiverse landscape. Additional loss of forest in the Amazon from infrastructure development and inundation from dams can have profound repercussions on the hydrology of the entire region. The Amazon serves as a sort of hydrological pump, recycling rainfall inland from the Atlantic coast. If forest loss, fragmentation, and drying increase to the point that the Amazon's ability to recycle rainfall weakens, not only will hydropower potential be reduced, but the entire ecosystem could be in jeopardy. The forest could be transformed from a major carbon storehouse to a major carbon emissions source.

An increasing share of hydropower investment is international. For example, Brazilian and Indian companies are building dams around the world. South Korean companies are investing in hydropower facilities in Pakistan. But no one is doing more hydropower internationally than China. After dam projects fell out of vogue by traditional development funders like the World Bank in the 1990s, Chinese lenders and businesses stepped in, and they now are involved in more than 200 hydroelectric projects in dozens of countries, according to data from the nongovernmental organization International Rivers. About half the projects are in Southeast Asia. In 2011, for example, the government of Laos granted Sinohydro access to the entire Nam Ou river basin, where it plans to develop seven dams.

The China Three Gorges Corporation, one of China's largest hydropower developers, is among the many Chinese firms taking dam-building experience abroad, with active projects in Pakistan, Myanmar, Laos, and Russia. As the market for new dams in China is becoming saturated, the company is also diversifying into new energy forms, importantly wind and solar. By 2020, the company expects its hydro projects to total 70,000 megawatts of installed capacity, with an additional 20,000 megawatts in wind farms and other "new energy."

As of late 2014, companies from China are vying with those from other countries, including Spain and South Korea (which is working with Canada), for development rights to a major project on the Congo River in Africa, one of the world's major remaining hydropower frontiers. Two dams, Inga 1 and 2, were built at the Inga Falls in western Democratic Republic of the Congo in 1972 and 1982. The new project, called the Grand Inga, has an enormous potential power generating capacity estimated at 40,000 megawatts.

If harnessed, this energy from the Congo River would dramatically expand Africa's electricity production. The World Bank, the African Development Bank, and other financiers are looking at the project as a way to support economic development, with the aim of raising living standards throughout the region.

On the one hand, the river's energy is renewable and abundant in an energy-starved part of the world. But on the other hand, groups like International Rivers point out that much of the electricity from the Grand Inga development will likely go to industry and far-off cities, rather than to the people of the Democratic Republic of the Congo, many of whom live in rural areas far from any sort of electric grid. Already South Africa has signed up to buy more than half of the electricity to be generated by the new project's first phase, the Inga 3 dam. Then there are the usual negatives associated with large dams, including the inundation of land, the associated displacement of people, and the disruption of river transportation. Another concern is that the Inga 1 and 2 dams have not been well maintained and are putting out only 40 percent as much power as initially anticipated. The World Bank is helping to fund their rehabilitation, but even that endeavor has run into delays and cost overruns. Building the world's largest dam complex in the world's poorest country, one perennially plagued by corruption, is not without risk.

Rachel Kyte, World Bank Group vice president and special envoy for climate change, believes the move away from hydro a decade ago, at a time when many were questioning its net contribution, was a mistake. Given the need for electricity in so many developing countries, she thinks funding hydro can be justified. That is certainly conceivable, but it is also quite possible that with solar generating costs dropping so low, it may be both cheaper and less disruptive to supply electricity in the developing world with solar energy rather than hydropower. Certainly the financial risks are smaller.

Though it has recently begun to reconsider large dams in a more positive light, over the last decade more than 60 percent of World Bank lending for water power has been for small-scale projects, including run-of-the-river facilities that set a turbine in the stream to capture the energy from flowing water without creating a reservoir. They have the advantage over large dams of requiring only small amounts of investment capital. In addition, the engineering work is relatively simple and the environmental impact from reservoir creation and the direct displacement of communities are both avoided. In contributing to meeting daily electricity demand at the grassroots level, small-scale hydro can help to reduce poverty and advance economic development.

China has been the leader in developing small-scale hydro, having started working on this several decades ago. Its total installed hydroelectric capacity comes to 249,000 megawatts. Of this, over 65,000 megawatts of generating capacity comes from 45,000 relatively small hydropower generating facilities of 50 megawatts or less.

As more plans for adding turbines to generate power from rivers come to fruition, the impacts of small hydro will likely become clearer. The cumulative impact of many small dams can be substantial, causing some hydrologists to liken it to "death from a thousand cuts." In northern India, a cascade of small dams has been linked to worsened flooding, for instance. Klement Tockner of the Leibniz Institute of Freshwater Ecology and Inland Fisheries in Berlin notes that "we are seeing huge numbers of small hydropower plants affecting lots of free-flowing rivers, but not delivering much power." Ultimately, small hydro still may be a powerful aid, particularly in the developing world, where there are 1.3 billion people without electricity and another billion with only erratic electricity supply, but only if it is done thoughtfully.

One question remaining is whether small-scale hydro development can minimize negative effects that dams often have downstream, which historically have exacerbated tensions among communities, particularly on rivers that cross national borders. China relies heavily on the Yangtze and Yellow Rivers and their tributaries for the bulk of its hydroelectric generation. But it also taps rivers that are important to other countries.

In November 2014, China completed the first phase of a hydroelectric project on the Brahmaputra River, which starts in Tibet. Despite assurances that the additional build-out will be run-of-the-river projects allowing for continuous river flow, the development raises concerns in downstream India and Bangladesh. India itself is looking at the possibility of adding several hundred new dams to its roster, largely in-stream projects in the Himalayan region, where most of the hydroelectric potential has yet to be developed. China also appears to be moving forward in developing hydropower on the Nu River (also known as the Salween). This river, which starts in Tibet and flows to Myanmar, is the largest remaining free-flowing river in China.

China's dam building on the upper reaches of the Mekong River, which ultimately flows through Myanmar, Laos, Thailand, Cambodia, and Viet Nam, stresses its relationships with its downstream neighbors, where some 60 million people depend on the river flow. In 2012, Vietnamese President Truong Tan Sang told Radio Free Asia that after some of the early dams were built, river water and underground aquifers "are seriously declining, while floods, sea level rises, high tides, coastal erosion...have been exacerbated." A decrease in water flow allows saline water to creep up the river, while the loss of sediment transport from dam blockages can shrink the Mekong Delta, one of the world's most productive rice-growing regions. The largest lake in Southeast Asia, Cambodia's Tonle Sap—a major source of protein in a country where people are highly dependent on fish—could shrink in size as more upstream dams are completed.

Not to be left out, however, Cambodia and Laos, with investment from Thailand, Malaysia, China, and Viet Nam, are also looking at adding a series of dams on the river. The bulk of the power generated would be exported to Thailand and Viet Nam, with only 10 percent designated for the host countries. Yet a study by the nongovernmental International Centre for Environmental Management indicates that development of other renewable sources of electricity, importantly solar, could well exceed the dams' potential power generation.

Another site of contentious water allocation is in the Nile River Basin, now home to 600 million people. Downstream Egypt staked its claim in a 1929 treaty with the then-British colonies of East Africa. In 1959, Egypt and Sudan signed the Nile Waters Agreement, which gave Egypt 75 percent of the Nile River's flow and gave Sudan 25 percent. Ethiopia, at the Nile's headwaters, was left out. Impounding the Nile River near where it crosses from

Sudan into Egypt is the well-known Aswan High Dam,
which has a generating capacity of 2,100 megawatts.
This hydroelectric capacity could be reduced when
the reservoir for the Grand Ethiopian Renaissance Dam
on the Blue Nile, the Nile River's major source, is filled.
Ethiopia—Africa's second most populous country, with
many of its 94 million people still mired in poverty—has
spent over $1 billion on the project that is projected to
cost at least four times as much, sacrificing other public spending and risking a tremendous debt burden. Its
goal is to triple the country's electrical generating capacity, allowing for electricity sales to neighboring countries.
China has leant Ethiopia $1 billion for a transmission
line, but most international lending for the project has
been dissuaded by Egypt's concerns about losing water.
Also competing for the Nile's water are countries acquir-
ing land in the Nile Basin for farming, including South
Korea, Saudi Arabia, and India.

Dam building, largely by upstream Turkey, has
also exacerbated water scarcity in Iraq and Syria. As of
2014, Turkey housed 478 hydroelectric power plants.
Another 160 were under construction, including the
443-foot high Ilisu Dam on the Tigris. The dam is part
of the Southeastern Anatolia Project, which is intended
to provide power and also irrigation water for some
6,500 square miles of land. Unfortunately its reservoir
will flood an estimated 121 square miles—including
Hasankeyf, a settlement that has been continuously
inhabited for some 12,000 years—while leaving downstream areas with less water.

In North America, water allocation conversations
between the United States and Mexico, which share the
large Rio Grande and Colorado Rivers, date back to the
late 1800s. In the hierarchy of water uses outlined in
their 1944 Water Treaty, electric power generation ranks

after domestic and municipal use and use for agriculture and livestock. Water for nature is omitted from the treaty obligations. Diversions and dams on the Colorado River have meant that in many years the flow is depleted before it reaches the sea. In 2014, for the first time, the two countries allotted an increased share of the flow for the environment, allowing the river to reach the Gulf of California. Scientists are monitoring the region to see if periodic water releases from dams can help restore riparian ecosystems.

The advantages of countries working together on energy projects can be seen quite clearly in Central America. Costa Rica, El Salvador, Guatemala, Honduras, Nicaragua, and Panama have recently completed the Central American Electrical Interconnection System—a 1,100-mile-long high-voltage line that ties their national grids into a single regional grid. It also allows for power trades with Colombia and Mexico. This market enlargement, which has facilitated exploitation of the wealth of falling water resources in the region, was funded in part by the Inter-American Development Bank.

Beyond rivers, other water-power operations involve capturing the energy in tidal currents and waves. Wave energy projects are still largely in the testing phases, with most activity in Europe and Asia. Many countries with coastlines have considered capturing the energy in ocean tides, but only two have thus far made serious headway in doing so. South Korea (with 254 megawatts of tidal generating capacity) and France (240 megawatts) together account for over 90 percent of the world's tidal-generated electricity. Canada, China, and the United Kingdom make up much of the remainder. Total world tidal power capacity at the start of 2014 was near 530 megawatts.

The German company Siemens estimates that some 250 million homes worldwide could eventually be powered by tidal currents. Scotland's proposal to harness tidal energy in the Pentland Firth is expected to supply 86 megawatts of generating capacity in the first phase, potentially growing to 398 megawatts. Canada and the U.S. Department of Energy are experimenting with a tidal turbine in the mouth of the Bay of Fundy off the coast of Maine. The Chinese government is setting up their largest tidal test project near Shanghai. Other water energy projects in the works in China include a 10-megawatt ocean thermal conversion power station to be built by global security and aerospace firm Lockheed Martin. This technology relies on the heat differential between warm surface waters and cooler deep waters to drive a turbine. In its early days, ocean thermal power is still costly, but it could eventually undercut offshore wind.

A more established water energy practice that has gained attention in recent years is pumped storage. This involves using excess electricity when demand is low to pump water uphill so that it can be used to generate electricity when needed. Facilities can be connected to existing hydroelectric generating plants or they can be stand-alone, closed-loop, off-river systems. Worldwide pumped storage capacity stands at more than 130,000 megawatts. More than 50,000 megawatts of capacity are in Europe, which is planning to add another 11,500 megawatts. Some of this will come from modifying older facilities and some from investing in new ones. Japan and China each have over 20,000 megawatts of pumped storage capacity, as does the United States. Proposed U.S. projects would more than double its capacity. One of the attractions of pumped storage is that it can be deployed nearly instantaneously to offset fluctuations in wind and solar energy. In doing so, it helps expand the amount of wind and solar that can be integrated into the grid.

In sum, hydropower supplies an impressive one sixth of the world's electricity. Yet rivers in countries that are fully industrialized are near dam saturation. For the low-income countries that have more untapped river power potential, other renewables may prove a more cost-effective bet. Many of the historical decisions regarding financing hydropower were made before low-cost solar and wind energy arrived on the scene. With solar, people can own and thus control their power source, giving them a direct hand in the development process. Hydropower will continue to be important, but most of the big dam building is in the past.

Data, endnotes, and additional resources can be found at Earth Policy Institute, www.earth-policy.org.

9

The Accelerating Transition

The energy economy that is now powered largely by coal and oil will be powered increasingly by solar and wind energy. During the last century the world relied heavily on coal mines and oil fields. This century is witnessing a shift to renewable energy.

Several forces are converging to advance this great transition. Economically, it is being driven by the falling costs of renewables. Technologically, it will be fostered by the ability to run vehicles on electrons instead of hydrocarbons. Socially, there is strong and growing public opposition to coal and nuclear power. And geologically, there are increasing limitations on the easy extraction of carbon-rich fossil fuels from the ground. These forces, coupled with limits on how much carbon the atmosphere can hold without the planet warming into a dangerously erratic climate regime, are presenting a challenge unlike any civilization has faced before.

The transition has many players. They include environmental groups, leading universities, forward-looking corporations and governments, and a committed collection of savvy investors. We are all stakeholders. In the broadest sense, everyone who breathes cleaner air, drinks cleaner water, and benefits from a more stable climate will come out on top as the energy transition proceeds. Rapid change is becoming a way of life. The very geography of the energy economy is changing. In the old one, the world was heavily dependent on oil, much of it concentrated in a few countries in the Middle East. For many importing countries, energy supplies were half a world away.

This century, as the world shifts to solar and wind, the energy economy is localizing. Our power source can be as close as the roofs over our heads. Instead of a small group of corporations and countries producing and controlling most of the world's energy, people everywhere will be in the energy business, meeting their own energy needs with solar panels.

Like any major transition from one era to another, there will be winners and losers. From a business vantage point, the companies that manufacture and install solar panels and wind turbines are expanding rapidly. For example, the market for solar panels is growing at a staggering 50 percent a year. As photovoltaic (PV) prices continue to fall, electricity markets are being turned upside down. In more and more places, electricity from solar panels is beating the average grid cost of electricity—and even coming in at half the cost or less. Old energy sources like coal are starting to lose out. As Amory Lovins of the Rocky Mountain Institute puts it, "Ordering new coal plants in the face of renewable mandates and emerging carbon trading is akin to buying up carriage-makers just as automobiles began to relieve London's horse-manure crisis."

The great transition involves changes within cities. This will mean a shift away from the near-total dependence on car ownership that dominated life in industrial countries over the last century, particularly in the United

States. The focus instead will move to car sharing, bike sharing, and walkable communities. Smart urban transport planning everywhere will focus on people instead of automobiles, systematically expanding not only the use of buses, subways, and commuter rail but also bike lanes, sidewalks, and bike and pedestrian trails.

As the need for cars diminishes and the world automotive industry shifts from internal combustion engines to electric motors that are three times more efficient, the market for oil will shrink. The pipelines that once linked oil fields with refineries will one day be worthless. Oil refineries will dwindle as the older, less-efficient ones are closed first. The corner gas station will be replaced by a battery recharging station for electric cars.

Government policies are still an important component of the energy transition. Governments have used several basic policy instruments to support the move to carbon-free renewable sources of energy. One is the feed-in tariff (FIT), which typically guarantees renewable energy producers—from rooftop solar owners to large-scale wind farm operators—grid access and a long-term purchase price for their electricity. By the start of 2014, some 70 countries, including many in Europe, were using FITs to encourage investment in renewables. In India, there are 14 state-level FITs in addition to a national one. Gujarat's feed-in policy, a prime component of its broader Solar Power Policy that went into effect in 2009, has helped crown it as India's leading solar state—with enough PV capacity as of early 2014 to power 825,000 Gujarti homes.

Another government measure is to mandate that a certain amount of electricity generation be from renewable sources. Called renewable portfolio standards (RPS) or quotas, these policies are in place at the national level in some two dozen countries. More than 50 states and provinces in various parts of the world have them as well, including 15 states in India and 29 states plus the District of Columbia in the United States. Iowa, which now gets more than 25 percent of its electricity from the wind, in 1983 enacted the first RPS anywhere in the world.

RPS policies in the United States generally require utilities to get anywhere from 10 percent to 40 percent of the electricity they sell from renewable sources, with California and Hawaii at the upper end of that range. In his early 2015 inaugural address, Governor Jerry Brown proposed that California strive to increase its renewables mandate from 33 percent by 2020 to 50 percent by 2030.

Tax credits are also used to support deployment of wind and solar power. U.S. wind power installations historically have soared in years when there was a wind energy production tax credit of a couple of cents per kilowatt-hour—and plummeted when Congress allowed the tax credit to lapse. And for solar power, an investment tax credit worth 30 percent of the installed cost of a residential or commercial rooftop system has helped spur the recent rapid spread of PV. Some 36 other countries also have national production or investment tax credits for renewable energy.

Such pro-renewables policies help level the playing field with artificially cheap fossil fuels that have been subsidized long past their debuts on the energy scene. The energy transition would be supercharged by systematically putting a price on carbon to convey more accurately the true social and environmental costs of burning coal, oil, and natural gas.

Done right, pricing carbon sends a powerful market signal and guides decisionmakers toward more-sustainable choices. Imagine the effect of incorporating fossil fuels' full costs to society in fuel prices. From the marring of landscapes to water and air pollution and climate change, we know that fossil fuel reliance is extraordinarily costly.

Putting a price on carbon can involve implementing a carbon tax, a cap-and-trade system, or a combination of the two. With cap-and-trade programs, regulators set a limit on emissions, and polluters can either reduce their emissions or buy emissions permits on the carbon market. The market sets the price.

A carbon tax, in contrast, is a far simpler instrument: a tax on each ton of carbon dioxide emitted. It could be applied at the wellhead or mine or at the point where fossil fuels are processed or used. Revenue from a carbon tax can go toward environmental, clean energy, or efficiency programs, can be offset by a reduction in taxes on labor, or can be returned to consumers directly via a dividend. A means of returning money to people helps ensure that most families, particularly lower-income ones, end up better off financially with the carbon tax than they were before.

Carbon taxes are widely endorsed by economists as a way to correct a market failure. N. Gregory Mankiw, who was Chairman of the Council of Economic Advisors under George W. Bush, writes that "cutting income taxes while increasing gasoline taxes would lead to more rapid economic growth, less traffic congestion, safer roads, and reduced risk of global warming—all without jeopardizing long-term fiscal solvency. This may be the closest thing to a free lunch that economics has to offer." Writing in the *Financial Times* in early 2015, former U.S. Treasury Secretary Lawrence Summers advocates a carbon tax in the United States, starting at $25 per ton of carbon dioxide (CO_2) (about 25¢ per gallon of gasoline), with revenue split between infrastructure improvements and labor tax credits.

Some 40 countries have either implemented or are planning national carbon pricing mechanisms, according to a May 2014 World Bank report. They typically target one or more economic sectors; the power and industrial sectors are nearly always included. The Bank counted a further 23 subnational jurisdictions pricing carbon. Seven regional cap-and-trade pilot programs are already under way in China, for example. When China rolls out its planned national cap-and-trade program in 2016, roughly a quarter of global carbon emissions will then be priced.

Critics often warn that carbon taxes and cap-and-trade systems will be an economic burden, but examples to the contrary abound. Ireland set a carbon tax on natural gas and oil consumption in 2010, covering roughly 40 percent of national greenhouse gas emissions. By 2013, emissions had dropped by some 6 percent, even as the economy grew. In May of that year, Ireland expanded its carbon pricing to include peat and coal. Former Energy Minister Eamon Ryan summed up the situation: "We just set up a price signal that raised significant revenue and changed behavior. Now, we're smashing through the environmental targets we set for ourselves."

The province of British Columbia in Canada implemented an economy-wide carbon tax of $10 per ton of CO_2 in 2008, rising to $30 per ton by 2012. By design, the tax is revenue-neutral: cuts in other taxes, such as income and business taxes, offset the rise in fossil fuel prices. Since the carbon tax went into effect, British Columbia's per person consumption of gasoline and other petroleum products has declined 15 percent—three times the national rate—while its economic growth has kept pace with the rest of the country.

In the United States, data through 2013 show that the nine northeastern and mid-Atlantic states belonging to the Regional Greenhouse Gas Initiative (RGGI) cap-and-trade program reduced their power sector emissions

18 percent since the system was launched in 2009. Over the same period their collective economic growth outpaced the other 41 states, where emissions fell just 4 percent. If the RGGI states continue to spend most of the revenue from pollution permit auctions on efficiency measures, they could reap a net economic benefit of $8 billion by 2020.

Indeed, investing in energy efficiency is generally a good economic bet. While it is exciting that wind and solar power are increasingly cost-competitive with fossil fuels and nuclear power, it is generally cheaper to invest in energy efficiency than to build new generating capacity. The International Energy Agency reports that in 2011, efficiency gains since the 1970s in 11 of its member nations—including Australia, Japan, Germany, and the United States—saved those countries more than $740 billion in avoided energy costs.

There is an enormous potential to reap substantial energy savings in each of the major energy-consuming sectors: lighting, buildings, appliances, industry, and transportation. For example, about 20 percent of global electricity consumption goes to lighting. If all the world's lightbulbs were switched from traditional incandescents to compact fluorescents, which use 75 percent less electricity, some 270 coal-fired power plants could shut down. This shift is already starting. Going further, replacing incandescents with LEDs (light-emitting diodes) can reduce electricity use by up to 90 percent. For perspective, replacing a single 100-watt incandescent bulb with an LED can save enough energy over the bulb's lifetime to drive a Toyota Prius hybrid-electric car from New York to San Francisco.

The world's most dynamic system for upgrading efficiency standards is Japan's Top Runner Program. In this system, which was introduced in 1999, the most efficient products marketed today set the standard for those sold in the future. Companies have 3–10 years to comply once a new standard is set. Depending on the technology, products have seen efficiency improvements of anywhere from 22 percent to 99 percent. Between 2005 and 2010, for example, refrigerators sold in Japan became 43 percent more energy-efficient. As of late 2014, some 30 product categories were subject to Top Runner standards, including air conditioners, computers, household appliances, industrial motors, lighting, and even light-duty cars and trucks. With the Top Runner Program continuing a decades-old commitment to energy efficiency in Japan, it is no wonder that consumers the world over associate Japanese automotive, appliance, and electronics brands with efficiency.

Some national governments are planning major changes to reduce fossil fuel use. India, for instance, wants to replace 26 million rather inefficient diesel- or grid-powered irrigation pumps with solar-powered pumps, potentially saving the government billions of dollars in fuel and electricity subsidies. The plan would require farmers to switch to highly efficient drip irrigation systems to qualify for the program, meaning that both fossil fuel and water use would drop. It is expected that these pumps will pay for themselves in one to four years. This massive prospective shift to carbon-free and water-efficient irrigation pumping is yet another building block in the new world energy economy.

The Indian government is also prodding several state-owned companies, including some in the fossil fuel and hydropower industries, to invest in solar power projects. Deploying large amounts of solar capacity will further reduce the cost of solar power through economies of scale. One of these companies, Coal India, which mines more coal than any other firm in the world, committed in late 2014 to set up 1,000 megawatts of solar projects in Andhra Pradesh, Telangana, and elsewhere. The agreement was signed with another state-owned firm, Solar Energy Corporation of India, which will build, operate, and maintain the plants.

Even oil-exporting Saudi Arabia, a desert country of 29 million people, is planning to harness its wealth of solar radiation in a big way. If the 41,000 megawatts of PV and solar thermal power plants that are operating, under construction, and planned were online today, Saudi Arabia could generate up to two thirds of its electricity from the sun.

Some European leaders in the energy transition are looking to go even further. Denmark, getting 39 percent of its electricity from the wind as of 2014, aims to bring this share to 50 percent by 2020. By 2035 all electricity and heat in that country should come from renewable sources. And by 2050 the goal is for all energy, including that used for transportation, to be renewable. In Scotland, a net exporter of electricity, renewable sources account for some 30 percent of electricity generation. The target for 2020 is for renewables to generate the equivalent of 100 percent of Scotland's electricity usage.

Ireland, now generating 17 percent of its electricity from wind, plans to get 42 percent from renewable sources by 2020, mostly wind power. Europe's largest economy, Germany, plans to increase its renewable electricity share from some 25 percent in 2013 to at least 40 percent in 2025. By 2050, Germany wants this to reach 80 percent.

Many cities are establishing their own ambitious goals for renewables—setting an example for national governments to move more boldly to phase out fossil fuels. San Francisco, for example, plans to get all its electricity from renewables by 2020 while it also moves to a zero-waste economy. Wellington, New Zealand, wants to get at least 78 percent of its electricity from renewables by that year. Munich, Germany, is aiming for 100 percent by 2025. Paris is planning to meet 25 percent of its total energy demand with renewables by 2020.

States are also propelling the energy transition. In Germany, four states now get half or more of their electricity from wind energy. Within the United States, Texas, California, Iowa, and South Dakota are providing wind power leadership. Japan's Fukushima prefecture, still recovering from the 2011 nuclear meltdown, has pledged to get 100 percent of its electricity and heat from renewables by 2040, partly by developing 1,000 megawatts of offshore wind capacity.

As of mid-2014, three provinces and three major cities in China have voluntarily committed themselves to reversing history by substantially reducing coal consumption by 2017. These include a 19 percent drop for Tianjin, 21 percent for Chongqing, and 50 percent for Beijing. These cuts could help China achieve its national goal of capping coal use by 2020 even sooner than that.

Although the planned reduction in coal use in China is both huge and unprecedented, the shift has rather obvious origins: the sheer effect of air pollution. For many—including the elderly, small children, and those with respiratory and cardiac illnesses—the pollution is so intense that breathing is literally life-threatening. Beijing has suffered through several major instances when pollution levels soared well beyond the margin of safety, termed "airpocalypses" by the media. As data on air pollution have become more widely available on the Internet, pressure for reducing coal use has intensified. Greenpeace China sums it up: "Citizens have started to demand a quality of life that cannot be measured in money—cleaner air and a healthier future for their kids. How long it will take to achieve truly clean skies in Chinese cities will be influenced by these agents of change."

Tired of living in cities where breathing is dangerous, people from all walks of life in China are demanding change on the energy front. China is now also getting a wakeup call from the market. New regulations designed both to improve air quality and stabilize climate are making it more difficult for coal burning to continue in a business-as-usual fashion. The *South China Morning Post* reported in July 2014 that financial bonds tied to China's coal mining industry were facing the prospect of default as coal use slows down.

Some banks are waking up to the fact that getting involved in the energy transition can yield strong returns. Large investment institutions, such as Morgan Stanley and Goldman Sachs, are channeling tens of billions of dollars into renewable energy. Stuart Bernstein, who coordinates Goldman's investment in this area, talks about "a transformational moment in time" as renewable energy takes off. Thinking long-term by investing in the transition to a cleaner energy future, he says, "will be important from a societal perspective, and it will be good business for us and our clients."

The commitment of several billionaires to carbon-free energy is a promising driver of the energy transition. Warren Buffett, the wealthiest member of this group, had invested some $15 billion in the development of solar and wind energy by early 2014. This includes a giant solar complex in California that will be the world's largest when completed in 2015. In June 2014, Buffett announced, "There's another $15 billion ready to go." Also investing in energy from the sun is Ted Turner, who has teamed up with Southern Power—a subsidiary of the coal-heavy energy firm Southern Company—to acquire seven solar power plants. Turner is also looking at the potential for investing in wind.

Denver-based Philip Anschutz, who made billions in oil and gas, is committed to the construction of a 3,000-megawatt wind farm in south-central Wyoming and also to building a transmission line that will carry wind-generated electricity over 700 miles to California, Arizona, and Nevada. For wind developers in Wyoming, a state with a wealth of wind resources but only 580,000 people, California's 38 million residents represent a very attractive market.

Michael Bloomberg, one of the most successful entrepreneurs of his generation and a former three-term mayor of New York City, is also helping speed the transition. His $50 million donation to the Sierra Club's Beyond Coal campaign in 2011 has strengthened efforts to close coal-fired power plants. But perhaps even more important than the money itself was the symbolic statement it made, given Bloomberg's status in the business world. When Michael Bloomberg says coal must go, people listen.

Bloomberg, an independent, also teamed up with fellow billionaire Tom Steyer, a Democrat, and Republican Hank Paulson, former Secretary of the Treasury under George W. Bush, to chair a project called Risky Business that is designed to quantify the economic risks associated with a changing climate. Steyer, a former hedge fund manager turned climate activist, has launched a nationwide climate education campaign in hopes of countering the people who deny that the climate is changing, and thus help mobilize support for an all-out effort to switch to carbon-free renewable energy.

Businesses turning to renewable energy are reaping savings. A number of leading corporations are lowering their electric bills with emissions-free on-site solar power. In 2014, telecom giant Verizon installed solar PV systems totaling 10 megawatts across eight of its facilities in California, Maryland, Massachusetts, New Jersey, and New

York. This $40 million investment nearly doubled the solar power capacity the company had installed since it launched an on-site energy program in 2013.

Walmart, America's largest retailer, is also pressing ahead. By late 2014 it had installed roughly 260 solar power systems on its U.S. buildings, each one generating 10–30 percent of the facility's electricity supply. The company's goal is to install up to 400 more PV systems at its U.S. facilities over the next four years. In May 2014, CEO Bill Simon described Walmart's move to go solar: "It's a business decision. The renewable energy we buy meets or beats prices from the grid." By taking its renewable energy and energy efficiency goals to its global operations, Walmart estimates that it will reap $1 billion per year in energy savings by 2020.

Each quarter, the U.S. Environmental Protection Agency (EPA) releases a ranking of companies, schools, and municipalities using green power. In late 2014, the top five firms were Intel, Kohl's Department Stores, Microsoft, Google, and Walmart. Intel, Kohl's, Staples, and Unilever were among the 600 entities that generated or purchased enough electricity from renewable sources to satisfy all of their electricity needs. Apple was not far behind, at more than 90 percent.

One of Google's most recent renewable energy investments, an 82-megawatt solar PV array in southern California, provides some powerful imagery of the energy transition. The solar project is being installed on an abandoned oil and gas field, where production had declined precipitously and was no longer profitable. So instead of creaking derricks pumping a dwindling supply of oil, this 700-acre site will soon feature solar panels silently turning the sun's energy into carbon-free electricity.

Among the large industrial companies increasing their use of renewable energy is the aerospace giant Boeing.

Almost half of the electricity it uses across its operations now comes from renewable sources, including hydropower. At Boeing's facility in North Charleston, South Carolina, renewables provide 100 percent of the electricity needed, either from the 10-acre rooftop PV array on an aircraft assembly building or from purchased renewable energy certificates.

Another large firm using renewables is the global building efficiency and automotive technology company Johnson Controls. Close to 20 percent of its electricity comes from renewable sources. The company is also shifting its vehicle fleet to more-efficient hybrids and electric vehicles. By 2013, it was saving $1.4 million per year in fuel costs.

The EPA also publishes a list of companies and institutions that sign long-term contracts for renewably generated electricity. Many are specifically for wind-generated electricity. A major benefit of these purchase agreements is that a company can get a guaranteed low price. Among the entities keen to buy green power are Google, with two 20-year contracts totaling a stunning 720 million kilowatt-hours per year, sourced from wind farms in Iowa and Oklahoma, and the state government of Illinois, with a 10-year contract for roughly 50 million kilowatt-hours per year.

The University of Oklahoma, which sees itself as a leader in the energy transition, buys enough renewably generated electricity to satisfy three fourths of its needs. This facilitated the construction of the 101-megawatt OU Spirit Wind Farm near Woodward, Oklahoma. And Oklahoma State University is now getting 71 percent of its electricity from wind farms. To the east, Ohio State University, one of the largest U.S. universities, gets 23 percent of its electricity from green sources. Its goal, an ambitious one, is to become a carbon-neutral campus.

Aside from shaping the needed policies, governments are also huge energy consumers themselves. The U.S. government occupies nearly 500,000 buildings of various sizes and has almost 600,000 vehicles. Because it is far and away the country's—not to mention the world's—largest consumer, spending some $500 billion per year for goods and services, it can use its purchasing power to accelerate the energy transition. Various regulations require its buildings, vehicle fleets, and electronics purchases to meet certain efficiency standards. Besides saving energy, this also saves taxpayer money.

In December 2013, President Barack Obama announced that the federal government would require that 20 percent of the electricity it uses come from renewable sources by 2020. This is a near tripling of the earlier goal of 7.5 percent. In an earlier address to Congress, Obama acknowledged the economic and geopolitical importance of the energy transition: "The country that harnesses the power of clean, renewable energy will lead the 21st century. And yet, it is China that has launched the largest effort in history to make their economy energy efficient. We invented solar technology, but we've fallen behind countries like Germany and Japan in producing it. New plug-in hybrids roll off our assembly lines, but they will run on batteries made in Korea."

The U.S. government is also moving the market by requiring increases in fuel efficiency for all vehicle manufacturers. In 2013, the average new car got 24 miles per gallon. By law, this will rise to 54 miles per gallon in 2025, a doubling in 12 years. Part of the fuel economy improvement will come from having more hybrid-electric or all-electric vehicles (EVs) for sale. Further helping to facilitate the transition to cars that run on electricity, the United States is offering, among other incentives, a federal tax credit of up to $7,500 to encourage the purchase of electric vehicles and plug-in hybrid electric vehicles (PHEVs). Additional tax credits in some states take that benefit even higher.

China, which got off to a slow start with electric cars, is now planning a major push. In 2013, its sales of all-electric cars totaled a meager 14,600 and the figure for plug-in hybrids was only 3,000. But with at least a dozen new electric car models coming to market in the next several years, China is expecting a huge jump in sales.

In Norway, the world leader in promoting electric vehicles, EV sales topped 6 percent of all car sales in 2013. In the Netherlands, where the government gives a 10–12 percent tax break for electric vehicle purchases and supports more than 400 charging stations, the figure was 4 percent. France uses fees on inefficient vehicles to fund rebates for electric vehicles. It will soon have 200 new charging stations along its highways as part of a European Union–supported pilot project.

Ultimately EVs and PHEVs will challenge the dominance of traditional gasoline- and diesel-powered vehicles, and this may happen sooner than most people realize. The global financial services firm UBS projects that by 2020 battery costs will be slashed in half, making electric vehicles cost-competitive with traditional cars. With annual savings of up to $2,400 expected on fuel costs, the electric car becomes the obvious choice.

Improving economics for solar power could also factor into the future of electric vehicles. As costs come down for both battery storage and home solar systems, UBS expects that in much of Europe the combination of rooftop solar power, battery storage, and electric vehicles will be extraordinarily attractive to the average customer. By 2020, the investment will pay for itself within six to eight years, after which electricity for home use and car charging is essentially free for the solar system's remaining lifespan, a dozen years or more. UBS forecasts conservatively that as it becomes easier to "fill up" with solar energy, 1 in every 10 new cars registered in Europe will be all-electric a decade from now.

The energy transition is also being assisted by a vigorous divestment campaign directed at coal, oil, and natural gas companies. This campaign, which originated with Bill McKibben and the group he co-founded, 350. org, has helped open a major new front in the effort to phase out fossil fuels. It found fertile soil on college campuses. Focusing initially on university endowments, it has expanded to include pension funds and individual investment portfolios. Increasingly, fund managers are being urged to sell stocks in coal, oil, and natural gas companies and to invest in the energy sources of the future.

As the public mood regarding our energy future changes, companies involved in the coal, oil, and gas industries will carry a stigma. Just as tobacco firms were stigmatized a generation ago because of the health-damaging effects of smoking cigarettes, fossil fuel companies will suffer because of their role in disrupting the earth's climate. While the anti-tobacco campaign focused on personal health, this one is tied directly to the future of civilization itself.

The energy transition amounts to a massive restructuring of the global economy. Initially this energy transition was driven by government incentives, but now it is also being driven by the market. With the market today favoring both solar and wind energy in many locations, the transition is accelerating, moving much faster than anticipated.

The recent growth of renewable energy generation in an expanding group of countries makes it clear that solar and wind energy are no longer fringe energy sources. If Denmark can get over half of its electricity from wind for an entire month, other wind-rich places can do the same. When wind eclipses coal on some days in the United Kingdom, we get yet another glimpse of what is possible. And when the electricity from wind farms overtakes that from nuclear power plants, as it has done in China, it becomes clear that wind is a mainstream source of energy.

Power systems everywhere will look different. They will be made up of millions of solar panels, in many cases tied into a smart and flexible grid getting power from wind turbines as well as from geothermal and hydroelectric projects. In one sense, developing countries have an advantage because they can take a shortcut to the new energy economy, building it as they develop. Just as they bypassed the need to install telephone wires and poles when they turned directly to cell phones, they can avoid the need for an electric grid by going directly to rooftop solar panels.

The biggest question facing civilization is, Will the energy transition proceed fast enough for the world to avoid catastrophic climate change? No one can say with certainty. Only time will tell. But exciting change is afoot. The industrial revolution set the stage for disrupting the earth's climate. This new energy revolution is setting the stage for stabilizing it. Ambitious renewable energy targets are being surpassed years ahead of schedule. National wind and solar power production records are routinely being shattered. As victories in shuttering coal plants mount, as new clean energy systems are built, and as transportation systems are electrified, a tipping point could be near.

The energy transition will change not only how we view the world but also how we view ourselves. With rooftop solar panels to both power homes and recharge car batteries, there will be a degree of personal energy independence not known for generations. Our relationship with the natural world will change from one where we are in conflict with nature to one where we are more in sync with it. Coal plant smokestacks that dirty the air and alter the climate will be replaced by solar panels on our rooftops and wind turbines turning gracefully in the distance. Welcome to the clean energy era.

Data, endnotes, and additional resources can be found at Earth Policy Institute, www.earth-policy.org.

Additional Resources

Climate, Carbon, and Stranded Assets

Atif Ansar, Ben Caldecott, and James Tilbury, *Stranded Assets and the Fossil Fuel Divestment Campaign: What Does Divestment Mean for the Valuation of Fossil Fuel Assets?* (Oxford, U.K.: University of Oxford, 2013).

Jessica Blunden and Derek S. Arndt, eds., "State of the Climate in 2013," *Bulletin of the American Meteorological Society,* vol. 95, no. 7 (July 2014).

T. A. Boden, G. Marland, and R. J. Andres, "Global, Regional, and National Fossil-Fuel CO_2 Emissions," in *Trends: A Compendium of Data on Global Change* (Oak Ridge, TN: Carbon Dioxide Information Analysis Center, 2013).

Carbon Disclosure Project, at www.cdp.net.

Carbon Tracker Initiative, *Unburnable Carbon*, at www.carbontracker.org.

Climate Progress Blog, at thinkprogress.org/climate.

Fossil Free, at Gofossilfree.org.

Global Carbon Project, at www.globalcarbonproject.org.

Kate Gordon et al., *Risky Business: The Economic Risks of Climate Change in the United States* (New York: 2014).

Intergovernmental Panel on Climate Change, *Climate Change 2014: Synthesis Report* (Cambridge, U.K.: Cambridge University Press, 2014).

Bill McKibben, "A Call to Arms: An Invitation to Demand Action on Climate Change," *Rolling Stone*, 21 May 2014.

World Bank, *State and Trends of Carbon Pricing 2014* (Washington, DC: 2014).

World Bank, *Turn Down the Heat: Confronting the New Climate Normal* (Washington, DC: 2014).

Coal

Carbon Tracker Initiative, *Carbon Supply Cost Curves: Evaluating Financial Risk to Coal Capital Expenditures* (London: September 2014).

Yuyu Chen et al., "Evidence on the Impact of Sustained Exposure to Air Pollution on Life Expectancy from China's Huai River Policy," *Proceedings of the National Academy of Sciences*, vol. 110, no. 32 (6 August 2013), pp. 12,936–41.

Paul R. Epstein et al., "Full Cost Accounting for the Life Cycle of Coal," *Annals of the New York Academy of Sciences*, vol. 1219 (February 2011), pp. 73–98.

Lesley Fleischman et al., "Ripe for Retirement: An Economic Analysis of the U.S. Coal Fleet," *Electricity Journal*, vol. 26, no. 10 (December 2013).

Christian Lelong et al., *The Window for Thermal Coal Investment Is Closing* (Goldman Sachs, July 2013).

Conrad Schneider and Jonathan Banks, *The Toll from Coal: An Updated Assessment of Death and Disease from America's Dirtiest Energy Source* (Boston, MA: Clean Air Task Force, September 2010).

Li Shuo and Lauri Myllyvirta, *The End of China's Coal Boom* (Greenpeace East Asia, April 2014).

Sierra Club, Beyond Coal, at content.sierraclub.org/coal.

Ailun Yang and Yiyun Cui, *Global Coal Risk Assessment: Data Analysis and Market Research* (Washington, DC: World Resources Institute, 2012).

Anthony Yuen et al., *The Unimaginable: Peak Coal in China* (Citi Research, September 2013).

Energy Efficiency

Advanced Energy Economy, *Advanced Energy Technologies for Greenhouse Gas Reduction* (Washington, DC: 2014).

Sara Hayes et al., *Change Is in the Air: How States Can Harness Energy Efficiency to Strengthen the Economy and Reduce Pollution* (Washington, DC: American Council for an Energy-Efficient Economy, 2014).

International Energy Agency, *Capturing the Multiple Benefits of Energy Efficiency* (Paris: 2014).

International Energy Agency, *Energy Efficiency Market Report* (Paris: 2014).

International Energy Agency, *Light's Labour's Lost: Policies for Energy-Efficient Lighting* (Paris: 2006).

Rocky Mountain Institute, at www.rmi.org.

Geothermal

Magnus Gehringer and Victor Loksha, *Geothermal Handbook: Planning and Financing Power Generation* (Washington, DC: Energy Sector Management Assistance Program, June 2012).

Geothermal Energy Association, at www.geo-energy.org.

Juliana Glenn and Benjamin Matek, *The Status of Geothermal Power in Emerging Economies* (Washington, DC: Geothermal Energy Association, October 2014).

Roland N. Horne and Jefferson W. Tester, "Geothermal Energy: An Emerging Option for Heat and Power," *The Bridge*, vol. 44, no. 1 (Spring 2014), pp. 7–15.

International Geothermal Association, at www.geothermal-energy.org.

John W. Lund and Tonya L. Boyd, "Direct Utilization of Geothermal Energy 2015 Worldwide Review," prepared for World Geothermal Congress 2015, Melbourne, Australia, 19–25 April 2015.

Joseph N. Moore and Stuart F. Simmons, "More Power from Below," *Science*, vol. 340, no. 6,135 (24 May 2013), pp. 933–34.

Árni Ragnarsson, "Geothermal Development in Iceland 2005–2009," presented at World Geothermal Congress 2010, Bali, Indonesia, 25–29 April 2010.

Jefferson Tester et al., *The Future of Geothermal Energy: Impact of Enhanced Geothermal Systems (EGS) on the United States in the 21st Century* (Cambridge, MA: Massachusetts Institute of Technology, 2006).

ThinkGeoEnergy, at thinkgeoenergy.com.

U.S. Department of Energy, Frontier Observatory for Research in Geothermal Energy (FORGE), at energy.gov/eere/forge.

Hydropower

American Rivers, at www.americanrivers.org.

Atif Ansar et al., "Should We Build More Large Dams? The Actual Costs of Hydropower Megaproject Development," *Energy Policy*, vol. 69, no. 2 (June 2014), pp. 43–56.

International Commission on Large Dams, at www.icold-cigb .org.

International Energy Agency, *Hydropower Technology Roadmap 2012* (Paris: 2012).

International Rivers, *State of the World's Rivers* (Berkeley, CA: 2014), at www.internationalrivers.org.

Ruud Kempener and Frank Neumann, *Tidal Energy Technology Brief and Wave Energy Technology Brief* (Abu Dhabi, United Arab Emirates: International Renewable Energy Agency, 2014).

Heng Liu, Lara Esser, and Diego Masera, eds., *World Small Hydropower Development Report 2013* (Vienna and Hangzhou, China: United Nations Industrial Development Organization and International Center on Small Hydro Power, 2013).

Andreas Maeck, "Sediment Trapping by Dams Creates Methane Emission Hot Spots," *Environmental Science and Technology*, vol. 47, no. 15 (25 June 2013), pp. 8,130–37.

U.S. Department of Energy, Energy Information Administration, "Hydropower Explained," at www.eia.gov/ energyexplained/index.cfm?page=hydropower_home.

Christiane Zarfl et al., "A Global Boom in Hydropower Dam Construction" *Aquatic Sciences*, vol. 77, no. 1 (1 January 2015), pp. 161–70.

Nuclear

Mark Cooper, *Public Risk, Private Profit; Ratepayer Cost, Utility Imprudence* (South Royalton, VT: Institute for Energy and the Environment, Vermont Law School, March 2013).

Henry Fountain, "Chernobyl: Capping a Catastrophe," *New York Times*, 27 April 2014.

International Atomic Energy Agency, *Power Reactor Information System*, database at www.iaea.org/pris.

Amory B. Lovins, "The Economics of a U.S. Civilian Nuclear Phase-out," *Bulletin of the Atomic Scientists*, vol. 69, no. 2 (March/April 2013).

Oliver Morton, "Special Report: Nuclear Energy—The Dream That Failed," *The Economist*, 10 March 2012.

Mycle Schneider and Antony Froggatt, *The World Nuclear Industry Status Report 2014* (Washington, DC: July 2014).

Union of Concerned Scientists, "Nuclear Power," at www.ucsusa.org/our-work/nuclear-power.

U.S. Nuclear Regulatory Commission, "Backgrounder on Chernobyl Nuclear Power Plant Accident," "Backgrounder on Nuclear Insurance and Disaster Relief," and "Backgrounder on the Three Mile Island Accident," at www.nrc.gov.

World Nuclear Association, at www.world-nuclear.org.

Oil and Natural Gas

Concerned Health Professionals of New York, *Compendium of Scientific, Medical, and Media Findings Demonstrating Risks and Harms of Fracking (Unconventional Gas And Oil Extraction)* (New York: 2014).

Russell Gold, *The Boom: How Fracking Ignited the American Energy Revolution and Changed the World* (New York: Simon and Schuster, 2014).

Robert W. Howarth, "A Bridge to Nowhere: Methane Emissions and the Greenhouse Gas Footprint of Natural Gas," *Energy Science and Engineering*, vol. 2, no. 2 (June 2014), pp. 47–60.

Mason Inman, "How to Measure the True Cost of Fossil Fuels," *Scientific American*, vol. 308, no. 4 (April 2013).

Michael Klare, *The Race for What's Left: The Global Scramble for the World's Last Resources* (London: Picador, 2012).

Renewable Energy—General

Bloomberg New Energy Finance, Multilateral Investment Fund, U.K. Department for International Development, and Power Africa, *Climatescope 2014: Mapping the Global Frontiers for Clean Energy Investment* (London: 2014).

Bloomberg New Energy Finance, United Nations Environment Programme, and Frankfurt School of Finance & Management, *Global Trends in Renewable Energy Investment 2014* (Frankfurt, Germany: 2014).

Database of State Incentives for Renewables & Efficiency, at www.dsireusa.org.

Mark A. Delucchi and Mark Z. Jacobson, "Providing All Global Energy with Wind, Water, and Solar Power, Part II: Reliability, System and Transmission Costs, and Policies," *Energy Policy*, vol. 29 (2011).

Justin Gillis, "Sun and Wind Alter Global Landscape, Leaving Utilities Behind," *New York Times*, 13 September 2014.

Greentech Media, at www.greentechmedia.com.

International Energy Agency, *Energy Technology Perspectives 2014* (Paris: 2014).

International Energy Agency, *World Energy Outlook 2014* (Paris: 2014).

International Renewable Energy Agency, *REthinking Energy 2014* (Abu Dhabi: 2014).

Mark Z. Jacobson and Mark A. Delucchi, "Providing All Global Energy with Wind, Water, and Solar Power, Part I: Technologies, Energy Resources, Quantities and Areas of Infrastructure and Materials," *Energy Policy*, vol. 29 (2011).

Lazard, *Lazard's Levelized Cost of Energy Analysis* (New York: 2014).

REN21, *Renewables 2014 Global Status Report* (Paris: 2014).

Sven Teske et al., *Greenpeace, Energy [R]evolution* (Washington, DC, and Brussels: Greenpeace and Global Wind Energy Council, 2014).

U.S. Environmental Protection Agency, "Green Power Partnership," at www.epa.gov/greenpower.

Ethan Zindler et al., *2014 Sustainable Energy in America Factbook* (Bloomberg New Energy Finance, 2014).

Solar

David Biello, "Solar Wars," *Scientific American*, vol. 311 (November 2014).

European Photovoltaic Industry Association, *Global Market Outlook for Photovoltaics 2014–2018* (Brussels: May 2014).

GTM Research and Solar Energy Industries Association, *U.S. Solar Market Insight*, quarterly and annual reports at www.seia.org/research-resources/us-solar-market-insight.

Franz Mauthner and Werner Weiss, *Solar Heat Worldwide: Markets and Contribution to the Energy Supply 2012* (Gleisdorf, Austria: International Energy Agency, Solar Heating & Cooling Programme, June 2014).

John Perlin, *Let It Shine: The 6,000-Year Story of Solar Energy* (Novato, CA: New World Library, 2013).

David Roberts, "Utilities for Dummies" series, at grist.org/series/utilities-for-dummies.

Vishal Shah, Jerimiah Booream-Phelps, and Susie Min, *2014 Outlook: Let the Second Gold Rush Begin* (New York: Deutsche Bank Markets Research, January 2014).

Solar Energy Industries Association, at www.seia.org.

UBS Ltd., "Will Solar, Batteries and Electric Cars Re-shape the Electricity System?" (Zurich: 20 August 2014).

U.S. Department of Energy, "2014: The Year of Concentrating Solar Power," fact sheet (Washington, DC: May 2014).

U.S. Department of Energy, SunShot Initiative, at energy.gov/eere/sunshot.

Transportation and Cities

Bike-Sharing World Map, at www.bikesharingworld.com.

Benjamin Davis and Phineas Baxandall, *Transportation in Transition* (Boston: U.S. PIRG Education Fund and Frontier Group, December 2013).

Tony Dutzik and Phineas Baxandall, *A New Direction: Our Changing Relationship with Driving and the Implications for America's Future* (Boston: U.S. PIRG Education Fund and Frontier Group, 2013).

Institute for Transportation and Development Policy, at www.itdp.org.

International Energy Agency, "Transport," at www.iea.org/topics/transport.

Janet Larsen, "Bike-Sharing Programs Hit the Streets in Over 500 Cities Worldwide," *Plan B Update* (Washington, DC: Earth Policy Institute, 25 April 2013).

National Complete Streets Coalition, at www.smartgrowthamerica.org/complete-streets.

John Pucher and Ralph Buehler, eds., *City Cycling* (Cambridge, MA: The MIT Press, 2012).

Susan Shaheen and Adam Cohen, *Innovative Mobility Carsharing Outlook* (Berkeley, CA: Transportation Sustainability Research Center–University of California, Berkeley, Summer 2014).

Michael Sivak, *Has Motorization in the U.S. Peaked?* (Ann Arbor, MI: University of Michigan Transportation Research Institute, 2014).

U.S. Environmental Protection Agency, *Light-Duty Automotive Technology, Carbon Dioxide Emissions, and Fuel Economy Trends: 1975 through 2014* (Washington, DC: 2014).

Wind

American Wind Energy Association, at www.awea.org.

Cristina L. Archer and Mark Z. Jacobson, "Supplying Baseload Power and Reducing Transmission Requirements by Interconnecting Wind Farms," *Journal of Applied Meteorology and Climatology*, vol. 46 (November 2007), pp. 1,701–17.

Global Wind Energy Council, *Global Wind Report: Annual Market Update 2013* (Brussels: 2014).

Xi Lu, Michael B. McElroy, and Juha Kiviluoma, "Global Potential for Wind-Generated Electricity," *Proceedings of the National Academy of Sciences*, vol. 106, no. 27 (7 July 2009), pp. 10,933–38.

Navigant Consulting, Inc., *Offshore Wind Market and Economic Analysis: 2014 Annual Market Assessment* (Burlington, MA: September 2014).

Christian von Hirschhausen, "The German 'Energiewende'—An Introduction," *Economics of Energy & Environmental Policy*, vol. 3, no. 2 (2014), pp. 1–12.

Ryan Wiser and Mark Bolinger, *2013 Wind Technologies Market Report* (Washington, DC: U.S. Department of Energy, Office of Energy Efficiency & Renewable Energy, August 2014).

Justin Wu, "BNEF University: How Innovation is Driving System Change," presentation at The Future of Energy Summit 2014, New York, 7 April 2014.

Index

Acknowledgments

My three coauthors—Janet Larsen, director of research, and my research colleagues J. Matthew Roney and Emily E. Adams—not only helped write this book, they did most of the research. Their years of experience with the many issues covered in this book were invaluable, particularly since the energy transition is driven by technologies that are advancing so fast. We were also assisted by research intern Lindsay Garten.

Because EPI deals with global issues and writes for a worldwide constituency, we are heavily dependent on an international network of publishers in 34 languages, including virtually all the major languages. Fortunately for EPI, the translation and publication into other languages is undertaken by our many publishing friends in other countries. As a result of their efforts, we now have nearly an entire bookcase filled with the many language editions of our first 13 books. They have singlehandedly multiplied our global effectiveness manyfold. We and the world are grateful to them.

On the administrative side are Reah Janise Kauffman, our vice president, who effectively directs the Institute's outreach effort; Millicent Johnson, our manager of publications sales, who serves as our office quartermaster and librarian; and Julianne Simpson, our web communications coordinator, who does our social networking and helps with outreach.

Those who helped by reviewing various drafts of the book or certain chapters include Bill Brown, Gail Gorham, Linda Harrar, Maureen Kuwano Hinkle, and Jessie Roberts. Further thanks goes to those who were helpful in providing specific information, including Kara Choquette, Scott Cohen, James Critchfield, Paul DeMaio, Brett Fleishman, Karl Gawell, Nicole Ghio, Justin Guay, Caroline Herron, Mary Anne Hitt, Doug Hollett, Rudhdi Karnik, Melissa Klein, Kim Kohl, Xiupei Liang, Kimberly Lucas, John Lund, Vrinda Manglik, Benjamin Matek, Russell Meddin, Shyam Mehta, Peter Midgley, Jay Nathwani, Liming Qiao, Surabhi Rajagopal, Alexander Richter, Anastasia Schemkes, Mycle Schneider, Jim Swafford, Carsten Vittrup, and Mark Wakefield.

As always, we are in debt to our editor, Linda Starke, with over 30 years of international experience in editing environmental books and reports. She has brought her sure hand to the editing of not only this book but all my books during this period.

The book was produced in record time thanks to the conscientious efforts of Maggie Powell, who prepared the page proofs under a very tight deadline. Similarly for the index that was ably prepared by Kate Mertes.

We are also indebted to our funders, including the United Nations Population Fund and the Farvue, Shenandoah, and Wallace Genetic foundations. For individual donors, I particularly would like to thank Fred Stanback, who has been such a generous supporter. We also benefit from ongoing support from Laney Thornton, Peter Seidel, and John Robbins.

Finally, my thanks to the superb team at W. W. Norton & Company, especially Amy Cherry, our book manager; Louise Parasmo, who put the book on a fast-track production schedule; Chin-Yee Lai, book jacket designer; Bill Rusin, Marketing Director; and Drake McFeely, President, with special thanks for his support. It is a delight to work with such a talented team and to have been published by W. W. Norton for 40 years.

And thanks to you, our readers, because the success of this book depends on you.

Lester R. Brown

About the Authors

Lester R. Brown is President of Earth Policy Institute, a nonprofit, interdisciplinary research organization based in Washington, D.C., which he founded in May 2001. The purpose of the Earth Policy Institute is to provide a plan for sustaining civilization and a roadmap of how to get from here to there.

Brown has been described as "one of the world's most influential thinkers" by the *Washington Post*. The *Telegraph of Calcutta* called him "the guru of the environmental movement." In 1986, the Library of Congress requested his papers for its archives.

Some 40 years ago Brown helped pioneer the concept of environmentally sustainable development, a concept embodied in Plan B. He was the Founder and President of Worldwatch Institute during its first 26 years. During a career that started with tomato farming, Brown has authored or coauthored 53 books and been awarded 25 honorary degrees. With books in more than 40 languages, he is one of the world's most widely published authors.

Brown is a MacArthur Fellow and the recipient of countless prizes and awards, including the 1987 United Nations Environment Prize, the 1989 World Wide Fund for Nature Gold Medal, and Japan's 1994 Blue Planet

Prize for his "exceptional contributions to solving global environmental problems." More recently he was awarded the Presidential Medal of Italy. He has been appointed to three honorary professorships in China, including one at the Chinese Academy of Sciences.

Janet Larsen is Director of Research and one of the incorporators of Earth Policy Institute. She manages the institute's research program and covers a range of trends from an interdisciplinary perspective, including energy, climate, population, water, and food. Previously she worked at Worldwatch Institute. Larsen holds a degree in Earth Systems from Stanford University.

J. Matthew Roney, Research Associate, joined Earth Policy Institute in 2007. He holds a BS in Environmental Conservation from the University of New Hampshire and an MS in Environmental Sciences and Policy from Johns Hopkins University. In addition to renewable energy and nuclear power, Roney's research topics include transportation, fisheries, and fish farming.

Emily E. Adams, Staff Researcher, joined Earth Policy Institute in 2012. She received a Master of Environmental Management degree from Duke University's Nicholas School of the Environment with a focus on the intersection of science and policy. Adams completed her undergraduate degree in Environmental Studies at American University.